LET THE RIVERS RUN

LIBRARY OF CHRISTIAN STEWARDSHIP

⋆ *Stewardship in Contemporary Theology*. T. K. Thompson, editor. New York: Association Press, 1960.

⋆ *Christian Stewardship and Ecumenical Confrontation*. T. K. Thompson, editor. New York: Dept. of Stewardship & Benevolence, National Council of Churches, 1961.

⋆ *Stewardship in Mission*. Winburn T. Thomas, editor. Englewood Cliffs: Prentice-Hall, 1964.

⋆ *Handbook of Stewardship Procedures*. T. K. Thompson. Englewood Cliffs: Prentice-Hall, 1964.

⋆ *The Christian Meaning of Money*. Otto A. Piper. Englewood Cliffs: Prentice-Hall, 1965.

⋆ *Stewardship Illustrations*. T. K. Thompson, editor. Englewood Cliffs: Prentice-Hall, 1965.

⋆ *Stewardship in Contemporary Life*. T. K. Thompson, editor. New York: Association Press, 1965.

⋆ *Why People Give*. Martin E. Carlson. New York: Council Press, 1968.

⋆ *Punctured Preconceptions*. Douglas W. Johnson and George W. Cornell. New York: Friendship Press, 1972.

⋆ *The Steward: A Biblical Symbol Come of Age*. Douglas John Hall. New York: Friendship Press, 1982.

⋆ *Christian Mission: The Stewardship of Life in the Kingdom of Death*. Douglas John Hall. New York: Friendship Press, 1985.

⋆ *Teaching and Preaching Stewardship: An Anthology*. Nordan C. Murphy, editor. New York: Friendship Press, 1985.

Imaging God: Dominion as Stewardship. Douglas John Hall. Grand Rapids: Eerdmans and New York: Friendship Press, 1986.

Public Theology and Political Economy: Christian Stewardship in Modern Society. Max L. Stackhouse. Grand Rapids: Eerdmans, 1987.

The Stewardship of Life in the Kingdom of Death. Douglas John Hall. Grand Rapids: Eerdmans, 1988 (revised edition of *Christian Mission*).

Stepping Stones of the Steward. Ronald E. Vallet. Grand Rapids: Eerdmans, 1989.

The Steward: A Biblical Symbol Come of Age (revised edition). Douglas John Hall. Grand Rapids: Eerdmans and New York: Friendship Press, 1990.

Let the Rivers Run: Stewardship and the Biblical Story. Eugene F. Roop. Grand Rapids: Eerdmans, 1991.

⋆ Title is out of print

Let the Rivers Run

Stewardship and the Biblical Story

EUGENE F. ROOP

William B. Eerdmans Publishing Company
Grand Rapids, Michigan

Printed in the United States of America

Library of Congress Cataloging-in-Publication Data

Roop, Eugene F., 1942–
    Let the rivers run: stewardship and the biblical story /
Eugene F. Roop.
        p.   cm.   — (Library of Christian stewardship)
    ISBN 0-8028-0609-0 (pbk.)
        1. Stewardship, Christian — Biblical teaching. 2. Bible. O.T. —
Criticism, interpretation, etc. I. Title. II. Series.
BS1199.S75R66   1991
248'.6 — dc20   91-26338
                                                         CIP

To my colleagues
of the
Ecumenical Center for Stewardship Studies
and the
Commission on Stewardship
of the
National Council of Churches of Christ
1980–1990

Contents

Foreword

I first had the opportunity to meet Eugene F. Roop at two events sponsored by the Ecumenical Center for Stewardship Studies (ECSS) in July 1987 at Stony Point Center, Stony Point, New York. The first of the two events was a colloquy for theological educators designed to acquaint them with biblical and theological roots of wider dimensions of Christian stewardship, dimensions that go beyond a limited understanding of stewardship as being solely congregational fund-raising. The second event was an educational event for stewardship leaders, most of whom were denominational stewardship staff members from across Canada and the United States. Some of the insights offered by Gene at those two conferences, and other insights as well, are now available to a wider audience through this book.

In his preface, Gene acknowledges that membership on the Board of Directors of ECSS nudged his biblical teaching and scholarship in a direction he never anticipated. It is my hope that *Let the Rivers Run* will help congregations in Canada, the United States, and other countries to move toward a more intentional grounding of stewardship in the Bible. The women and men, children and youth who sit in congregational pews are, in many cases, unsung heroes and heroines of the Christian faith. *Let the Rivers Run* provides an excellent opportunity for such insights to become incorporated into their ongoing daily lives. This process will be facilitated by the set of questions for further study and reflection found at the end of each chapter and by the excellent bibliography.

Gene has a special knack for taking stories from the Bible that we may have heard many times before and using them as lenses to help us see new dimensions of Christian stewardship. This is a gift of God to Gene, and one for which I am extremely grateful. This book, and especially its powerful final chapter which describes three biblical rivers, has the potential to transform the lives of individuals and corporate structures such as Christian congregations, denominations, ecumenical structures, and others. The three rivers are the river of creation, the river of righteousness, and the river Jordan. The call to become faithful stewards of the three rivers is compellingly presented.

I am tempted to expound on those three rivers and their significance for our lives, for the church, and for the world, but I will let Gene's words speak for themselves. May God bless you the reader and all those who turn to these pages. May you become a steward of the three rivers.

Ronald E. Vallet

Preface

Membership on the board of the Ecumenical Center for Stewardship Studies (ECSS) has nudged my biblical teaching and scholarship in a direction I never anticipated. This happened in part because those responsible for stewardship programming at the National Council of Churches relentlessly pursued conversation with those of us involved in theological education — even though they did not find us very eager conversationalists, at least not initially. Hopefully that has changed and will continue to do so.

Let the Rivers Run is intended to promote in local congregations exactly what ECSS fostered in me, a more intentional grounding of stewardship in the Bible. Hence the book is designed to facilitate study by groups in local congregations or other settings. Each chapter can be read quickly and — I hope — easily. The discussion anticipates that the reader will have some familiarity with the narratives in Genesis, Exodus, Deuteronomy, and Joshua. Readers are encouraged to read the biblical texts which correspond to the focus of each chapter before beginning the chapter itself. At the conclusion of each chapter the reader will find a set of questions for further study and reflection, and a selected bibliography is included at the end of the book to provide additional resources for study.

This book concentrates on specific texts from the Hebrew Bible, which Christians have called the Old Testament, because that is the center of my study. However, the discussion also includes frequent reference to and connections with the New Testament. As the reader will see, the New Testament depends on its Hebrew companion to identify and define the role of the steward.

Let the Rivers Run begins by looking at how the Bible has been used in North American churches as we have developed an understanding of Christian stewardship. Chapter two turns to the creation narratives in Genesis 1 and 2, texts which describe God's appointment of humankind as steward of the earth. Chapters three and four look at occasions of unfaithful, even sinful abuse of God's trust as reflected in the narratives of Genesis 3 to 11.

The next two chapters explore covenant in the Bible. Covenant provides an important biblical way to describe our responsibility as stewards. Chapter five discusses the distinctive covenant of gift and responsibility, associated in the biblical tradition with Moses and Sinai. Chapter six examines a second covenant tradition, the promissory covenant, connected in the biblical narratives with several key figures, among them Sarah and Abraham.

Chapter seven features the story of Joseph, who in many ways mirrors all stewards. At times Joseph acts as a model steward, but at other times his own interests interfere with his good judgment. In addition, this narrative serves as an important stewardship story because both God and nature function as stewards along with Joseph. At times their action supports Joseph, the model steward; at other times they soften the consequences of the steward's poor judgment. The eighth and final chapter turns to the biblical metaphor from which the book gains its title: the river. The chapter follows three biblical rivers which symbolize particular aspects of our responsibility as stewards made in the image of God.

My colleagues at ECSS and the Commission on Stewardship have convinced me that the biblical office of steward provides one of the most vibrant ways we can image the Christian role in God's world. For that and so much more I thank them. This book is the product of their instruction and encouragement as much as my efforts. I want especially to thank Nordan Murphy and Ronald Vallet, executive directors of ECSS and the Commission on Stewardship as well as good friends.

Eugene F. Roop

1. Stewardship and the Bible

The issues of Christian stewardship constantly change as the steward finds herself or himself in a changing world. Quite naturally, the Christian takes these new questions into conversation with the Bible, finding there possibilities and perspectives not seen by previous listeners to the Bible. One needs only to recall either from memory or through study the changes that have occurred in the twentieth century to realize that we use the word *stewardship* differently than our predecessors of only one or two generations. Nevertheless, throughout all those changes, the church has tried to listen to the Bible as well as respond to culture in defining and programming stewardship.

A glance at the literature from just the past few decades reveals the dramatic changes in stewardship curriculum for children and programming for adults. However, conversation with the Bible has remained a constant feature of stewardship education and action. We have taught children very early that stewardship is connected with our reading of the Bible. I remember the central place given to the words of the Bible as the church attempted to instill a notion of financial stewardship in me

1

as a child. I can still hear my Sunday school teacher encouraging me to give joyfully ten percent of my allowance to the church, for "God loves a cheerful giver." I assumed that meant I should smile when the offering basket was passed. While the basic commitment to a biblical foundation has not changed, the way in which we have worked with the Bible in understanding stewardship has shifted.

At first blush it might seem easiest if stewardship in the Bible could be reduced to a law — for example, a law that all Christians must give a certain percentage of income to the church, as is inscribed in my childhood memory. Obviously, some Christians interpret the Bible as providing such a scriptural mandate. This "law" would need to be enforced by ecclesiastical or even by civil authorities. However, most of us are reluctant to use the Bible in that way for several reasons. Fundamentally, such a program moves the church toward legalism, making law the primary category of biblical interpretation. As such, duty becomes the primary impulse for stewardship. Eventually emphasis on obligation erodes the heart of the gospel.

But what may at first seem like a bane also functions as a blessing. Because we do not have a simple categorical imperative, the Christian community is invited to ponder its stewardship role more comprehensively than would likely be necessary if the matter were covered by a scriptural law.

However, before we rush into the present discussion, we would do well to glance at the road traveled by "stewardship" in the church in North America. Only a few generations ago, stewardship was in fact decided by law, civil as well as ecclesiastical.

2

VOLUNTARY GIVING TO THE CHURCH

It does not overstate the case to say that stewardship programming in the church, as we are using the term, has been the distinctive product of the North American church. That is not to claim that none of the elements of what we call stewardship existed in the Christian church before the North American experiment. The emphasis on voluntary giving to support the community of faith was championed by dissenting groups such as the Anabaptists, the Quakers, and the Pietists, and later by the Methodists and the Baptists, before they immigrated to North America. Nevertheless, stewardship as the voluntary responsibility of members for providing the resources of the church has become the dominant approach of the whole Christian body because of the North American Protestant church.

It was not that way at the beginning. Many of the early European settlers in North America carried with them the principle of an established church, one in which all the members of a territory were required to be members of the church. The basic resources of the church came from taxes collected by the civil authorities. The idea of voluntary support of the church, or the "free church" ideal, entered the American scene primarily through those groups in Europe who had rejected the established church doctrine. Of course, some of the immigrants who brought the "established church" tradition to North America also viewed the church as a voluntary organization voluntarily supported by its members. Nevertheless, both in Canada and in the United States, the initial church organization of those connected with legally established churches in Europe included laws to support those churches by taxation in the "New World" as in the "Old."

Even after civil taxes were no longer used to support the churches — and this did not end in every place at the

3

same time — many churches continued to derive much of their income from the "pew tax" or "pew rental." This revenue system persisted into the twentieth century, although by the latter part of the nineteenth century most denominations, if not every congregation, had given up "pew rental" and had turned to the voluntary offering for revenue. Few of the historic so-called "free churches" ever had the "pew rental" system.

Most denominations, both from "free" and from "established" church backgrounds, had voluntary collections. However, when the bulk of the revenue came from required sources (taxes, pew rental, etc.), "freewill" offerings were frequently used for special causes such as benevolence societies ministering to the poor and/or support of new or poor churches (later for "foreign" missions). From the earliest days some revenue for the churches came from lotteries, games of chance in which some prizes were given away but most of the money was kept for the church. These games of chance usually involved chance drawings, and they seem to have been adopted by the church from games found at carnivals. Ironically, today civil authorities use lotteries and most Protestant churches refuse to support them.

A program of financial stewardship depending almost entirely on the voluntary gifts of church members became the norm for all churches in the latter half of the nineteenth century. Even those church groups that have "fund-raisers," which may include games of chance like bingo, draw most of their support from the voluntary contributions of church members. Hence, the "free church" perspective of the dissenting churches eventually became the "established" principle for all denominations in North America. The same is true for the so-called "mission" churches of Africa, Asia, and South America. It is within that victory of the "free" or "voluntary" principle that our theology of stewardship has developed in the twentieth century.

APPROACHES TO STEWARDSHIP AND THE BIBLE

In order to sharpen our understanding of the current state of the biblical grounds for stewardship, let us look briefly at some of the various ways the North American church has used the Bible to understand stewardship in the decades of the twentieth century. All of these approaches have developed in an ethos which assumes the "voluntary" principle of contribution to the church.

The "Golden Text" Approach

I have already mentioned one approach from my childhood. The church has gathered together a collection of pertinent "stewardship" texts that can be used to reinforce the responsibility of each individual to support the church financially. These might better be called "offertory texts." Several of these texts appear weekly in the offertory liturgy of the church:

> Set aside a tithe — a tenth of all that your fields produce each year. Then go to the one place where the LORD your God has chosen to be worshiped. (Deut. 14:22-23a, TEV)

> Give to others and God will give to you. Indeed, you will receive a full measure, a generous helping, poured into your hands — all that you can hold. The measure you use for others is the one that God will use for you. (Luke 6:38, TEV)

Each of you must give as you have made up your mir ,,
not reluctantly or under compulsion, for God lov ,s a
cheerful giver. (2 Cor. 9:7)

This "golden text" approach has proven valuable in
incorporating financial stewardship, most particularly the
Sunday "offering," into the flow of the liturgy of the
church. As such we must not undervalue it. Nevertheless,
this use of the Bible lifts words and sentences out of their
biblical context for use in worship. Sometimes, as with
Deuteronomy 14, for example, such an approach distorts
the meaning of the sentence in its biblical context. While
this approach is liturgically acceptable and furnishes "proof
texts" which reinforce some of what we want to say about
stewardship, we must conclude that this "golden text"
approach provides little in the way of solid footing in the
Bible.

The Historical Approach

In addition to the liturgically based "golden text" approach
to the Bible, the Christian church has used a historical
approach to establish a biblical foundation for stewardship
programs and practice. In this historical approach, scholars
and pastors have studied the financial practices and giving
patterns of ancient Israel and the early church, hoping to
find historical analogies and precedents. This investigation
has been fruitful in that it has shown that we are not the
first Christians to attend to the financial needs of the
community of faith. The earliest observations we have
from the New Testament church include reflections on
financial matters (Acts 2:44-45; 1 Cor. 16:1-2). However,
historical study has been less valuable in showing us exactly
how stewardship ought to be carried out today, given the

vast difference between our world and the socioeconomic systems of the ancient Near East and Roman Palestine.

Undoubtedly members of the community in ancient Israel were expected and probably even legally required to bring ten percent of their income to the sanctuary. That expectation was not eliminated in the New Testament, and it may even have been reinforced. However, the cultural and religious milieu has changed significantly with the end of a political system in which the faith community and the political community were the same. In addition, the Bible reflects differing perspectives concerning required support of the religious institutions. While the priestly and royal groups insisted that a tithe be brought to the sanctuary, some prophets and sages objected to the practice. They saw the religious institutions as unimportant or unworthy of support.

The New Testament suggests that Jesus was critical of some "stewardship" practices in his day — for example, the "corban" (see Mark 7:11). This ancient version of an annuity plan permitted individuals to give their estate to the temple and continue to use it during their lifetime. However, abuse of the system allowed people to evade their responsibility to assist their family members financially, especially aging parents, since they could insist that as faithful stewards they had given all to the sanctuary.

Although Jesus criticized the abuse of the "corban," this does not necessarily mean that he would disapprove of the annuity — our version of the "corban" — today. Economic situations and family relationships in North America today differ dramatically from those of Roman Palestine. This is just one illustration of the problem of using historical study of biblical times to ground our stewardship theory and practice. Identifying the financial practices of ancient Israel and the early church seldom translates easily into a program for our time.

At times we have been guilty of carefully crafting

7

historical pictures of the New Testament church or ancient Israel's temple so as to advance a stewardship program that we want in our churches. These "pictures" of the past have a promotional purpose rather than a historical one; they seek to promote a current stewardship program by appealing to the past. Such selective portraits emphasize certain similarities between the past and the present, with the hope that people will not notice the dissimilarities. For example, such promotional use of biblical history usually ignores the drastic disparity between the village peasant and theocratic urban economy of the ancient world and the secular international economy of our world.

Historical study of the Bible can provide us with much-needed information on how biblical communities struggled with issues of stewardship in their day. Examinations of Bible times that do not distort the past in the interest of the present agenda can provide a magnificent portrayal of the community of stewards. Such a portrait exhorts us to accept the mantle of steward handed on from our ancestors, but it does not proscribe what the Christian steward should be today.

Stewardship and Mission

We will take time to explore only one other way in which stewardship programming has worked with the Bible before turning to the most recent biblical study. In the past few decades, first informally and recently more formally, denominations have sought to tie the financial support of the church directly to the larger mission of the church. With this approach, Christians are encouraged to understand stewardship as engagement in the work of the church rather than as a duty to give to the church. This has provided a theology in which people give money out of their participation in the mission of the church rather than out of guilt, obligation, or duty.

This mission-based stewardship theology has required a different grounding in the Bible. Stewardship leaders have expanded their biblical exploration to include the mission texts of the church. At its best this has produced an exciting interface between giving and doing, steward-ship and mission, with a careful biblical foundation for mission. Admittedly, sometimes the result has been little more than a revision of the "golden text" approach, ex-panding the pool of "golden texts" to include mission slogans such as these:

> Truly I tell you, just as you did it to one of the least of these who are members of my family, you did it to me. (Matt. 25:40)

> The kingdom of God is not food and drink but righteousness and peace and joy in the Holy Spirit. The one who thus serves Christ is acceptable to God. (Rom. 14:17-18)

> Go therefore and make disciples of all nations, baptizing them . . . and teaching them to obey everything that I have commanded you. (Matt. 28:19-20)

> What does the LORD require of you
> but to do justice, and to love kindness,
> and to walk humbly with your God? (Micah 6:8)

Regardless of the pros and cons, tying stewardship together with a biblically grounded understanding of mis-sion has been enormously successful, so much so that most Protestants take it for granted. It is worth remember-ing, however, that the mission of the church has been defined quite differently by denominations and pseudo-denominational enterprises, a difference visible by comparing the mission statement of a Christian denomination with that of the major televangelists.

The Steward

In the past several decades, study of the Bible in connection with stewardship has taken still another direction. Scholars and church leaders have undertaken the task of redefining *stewardship* so that the word does not refer narrowly to the financial support of the denomination — or even support of the mission of the church — but places both mission and money into a still broader context. Douglas John Hall's book *The Steward: A Biblical Symbol Come of Age* has given a major boost to this new approach. Hall takes from the Bible not a text, a program, or a law, but a symbol or metaphor — the steward.

We will explore this more recent approach to biblical interpretation and Christian stewardship in some detail in the following chapters. As we do so, it will be helpful to remember the other approaches to stewardship and the Bible discussed in this chapter, for the purpose of this first chapter has been to recall some of the journey traveled up to this point. We must pay careful attention to the journey of our predecessors in stewardship if we are to avoid mistakes on the path ahead.

Questions for Discussion and Reflection

1. Recall for one another some of your earliest memories associated with Christian stewardship. For some of you this will

be from childhood, for others it may be when you first became a member or active member of the church.

2. Identify different ways you have seen the Bible used in stewardship programs in your congregations. Which seem appropriate to you and which trouble you?

3. Have we overdone the "free" or voluntary church principle? Do you think a minimum financial requirement for Christian stewardship should be established for all members? Where would you go to extract such a law from the Bible? How would you enforce it?

4. How do you feel about some of the non-offering ways of raising revenue for the church — e.g., bazaars, bingo, dinners, auctions? How do these revenue methods fit in with your understanding of the Bible?

2. The Appointment of a Steward: Genesis 1 and 2

It is likely that the word *stewardship* has never been limited to the economic realm of church activities. Perhaps that limitation has come about as a function of popular usage, narrowing the meaning of the word for everyday use. Nevertheless, for almost all of us, something to do with economics first comes to mind when we hear the word *stewardship*.

The agenda for a much broader discussion of stewardship is frequently traced to a statement by Charles Stoughton in 1940: "[Stewardship] is what I do after I say, 'I believe.'" This broad definition of stewardship received renewed emphasis in the 1960s, especially under the urging of T. K. Thompson, Executive Director of the Department of Stewardship in the National Council of Churches. Writers such as T. A. Kantonen, Helge Brattgard, and Frederick Herzog insisted that stewardship involves the fundamental Christian responsibility for God's world. Money management constitutes a crucial part of that responsibility, but not the only part. These writers discussed issues of justice and evangelism as much as offerings, care of God's creation as well as care of the church building.

12

It may be a result of our deafness that for the most part they went unheard. Thus it is ironic that we presume most of our Christian ancestors thought stewardship concerned only money management, but we have discovered a broader definition!

We have no right to expect that this generation will listen to us any better than we listened to our predecessors. Nevertheless we find ourselves insisting, like others before us, that stewardship has to do with the human role in the care of God's human and nonhuman world, which includes but is not limited to church finances.

As mentioned in the previous chapter, the agenda for this generation's exploration of stewardship has been set by Douglas John Hall's book, *The Steward: A Biblical Symbol Come of Age* (Grand Rapids: Eerdmans, 1990). Hall wants to expand the narrow view of stewardship as a particular church program or as obedience to specific scriptural mandates. Stewardship is much more comprehensive than that. Hall sees the steward as a biblical metaphor describing the responsibility of all humankind for the care of God's world, including financial resources and soil, human community and the gospel.

Obviously, steward is not the only metaphor for the Christian life. "Disciple," "priest," and "servant" are other biblical words which identify the Christian. But "steward" as a metaphor for the Christian life has a flavor all its own and is especially important. The role of steward has an equal measure of accountability and responsibility. As Hall notes, "the steward is not the master . . . and therefore is accountable. The steward is given a vocation to fulfil and the wherewithal to fulfil it, and therefore is responsible" (p. 235).

Before moving too far into the discussion of the steward metaphor, however, we must clarify how *metaphor* is understood in this discussion. A metaphor uses a familiar

13

word to create a picture for the reader. The reader is then asked to carry this familiar word picture over to another situation, one much less familiar. Through the use of a familiar word as a metaphor, we can portray some of what goes on in another less familiar arena. In using "steward" as a metaphor, we are borrowing the term "steward" from the political and economic world of ancient Israel and the early church in order to use it to picture some dimensions of the human role in God's world in our time. The match will not be exact, but there should be sufficient commonality that this biblical term can help us understand the relationship between God, humankind, and the world, a relationship we find hard to describe without "picture" words.

In order for a word to function well as a metaphor, a second aspect is needed. The word must spark the imagination of those who hear it. We must be caught up in the image at an emotional level for the metaphor to "work" for us. It is not enough that the metaphor provides a good analogy; it must also energize the imagination.

"Shepherd" has been one of the Bible's most captivating metaphors. Generations of listeners have been caught up by the image in the Psalmist's words, "The Lord is my shepherd." Therefore shepherd continues to function as an exciting metaphor even though most of us are miles and decades away from such a pastoral scene.

The metaphor of steward, although just as available, has not been used as frequently as many other biblical images. Nevertheless it seems to fit the distinctively new situation of the "free church" or voluntary stewardship ethos. "Steward" pictures a person working on behalf of and under the direction of another. Unlike a servant, however, a steward is one with the responsibility to exercise his or her own judgment and the authority to act. The effect of this shift from traditional stewardship

14

programming to the biblical metaphor of steward has been dramatic. It has opened up new ways of working with the Bible to ground stewardship. Instead of seeking biblical support for the stewardship program of the church, we are beginning to explore a new reading of the Bible in light of the steward metaphor found there.

Biblical study has been successful in showing that steward is indeed an available metaphor in the biblical texts. The picture of a steward that has emerged from study of Joseph, Daniel, the parables of Jesus, and the Greek word *oikonomos* has provided a colorful and expansive image, energetically calling people to care for human and nonhuman life and the earth which is home to all.

Although the word *steward* is not everywhere used in the biblical texts, its emergence from the biblical pages has permitted us to take a next step. Having established the presence and power of this biblical metaphor, we are now free to explore ways in which many biblical texts add flesh to the image of steward. At the same time the metaphor provides an avenue allowing us to move back and forth between the Bible and the human role in God's world.

GENESIS 1

It seems quite rare in our time that consensus develops among scholars about anything. Perhaps it has always been that way. Be that as it may, a consensus has emerged in stewardship study that Genesis 1 and 2 function as a critical starting place at which to enter into dialogue with the Bible about stewardship. While consensus does not mean unanimity, it does establish an agreed base on which we can build, a base that does not need to be constantly reset.

Therefore we will begin our discussion of the steward with the first chapter of Genesis.

Most of us know Genesis 1 well. We may not have it memorized, but the words are nearly that familiar. Although a more complete exploration of the steward metaphor would need to look at all of Genesis 1, we will concentrate on the blessing of God on humanity in 1:28. Stated boldly, the blessing of humanity in Genesis 1:28 provides a mandate for human stewardship:

> God blessed them and said to them, "Be fruitful and multiply, fill the earth and manage it; assume control over the fish of the sea and over the birds of the air and over every living thing that moves upon the earth." (my translation)

This text uses royal language to describe God's empowerment of humankind, designating humanity as manager in the world. Looking at the vastness of the universe, the Psalmist marvels at this divine decision:

> What is humanity that you attend to them . . . ?
> Yet you have made them little less than divine. . . .
> And you have put them in charge of the works of your hand. (Ps. 8, my translation)

Obviously, if the text stopped there we would have a mandate that unleashed human power in the world without check or qualification — a situation that many feel has happened. But being called as a steward does not provide a license to destroy creation.

In Genesis 1 the phrase "image of God" functions to check and channel this human mandate. Laying aside for the moment the many other possible meanings of the phrase "image of God," at the very least in this text the phrase limits the human mandate to take charge of the earth. Humanity is empowered to manage creation in the image of God. To understand what it means to manage and control, to subdue and have dominion — or whatever other translations we wish to use — we must understand God's management policies. When the steward wants to know how to use the power at human disposal, she or he must ask how God uses power. This text says nothing about management without reference to the board of directors, the divine council to whom God said, "Let us make humankind in our image" (1:26).

Genesis 1 portrays the human stewardship mandate using language which in its time was royal and in our time takes us into the corporate board room. That language has bequeathed to us both potency and problems. The mandate empowers the human community to actively engage in shaping the world. Our energy to work, manage, shape, envision, and implement comes as a gift from the Creator. However, that kind of empowerment — whether in the corporation or in the crown — has a way of losing touch with the one to whom it is accountable, soon inventing justification for whatever the manager wishes to do.

GENESIS 2

Because of the problematic language of Genesis 1, it seems fortuitous if not providential that the next chapter, Genesis 2, describes the human mandate using quite different language. Instead of seeing the man and woman as corporate executives, in chapter 2 we find them portrayed as gardeners: "Yahweh God took and placed '*adam* in the garden of Eden to cultivate and to care for it" (Gen. 2:15, my translation). Even at the emotional level we sense the difference in Genesis 2. God, the potter, stoops down and gathers up some dirt and gently forms a creature of the earth, breathing life into it. God places *'adam,* the human being, into a marvelous environment with water and rich soil, with freedom and companionship. The gentle Creator assigns to humankind a serving role: they are to cultivate the garden and care for it.

We must add that this narrative does not portray humanity simply as a slave. God assigns the naming task to *'adam,* which involves organizational responsibilities. *'Adam* is to put things in order in the garden. Nevertheless, there remains the clear picture that humanity is portrayed in the garden using serving rather than controlling language.

In a deep sense, the two narratives are saying the same thing: God has mandated humanity to take charge of the world. But the difference between the two narratives — between management language and servant language — is critical. Therefore it is fortunate that both are present. The image of the steward emerges within the dialogue between the management model of Genesis 1 and the servant role of Genesis 2. In both cases, the role of a steward blends the authority to carry out the vocation with the responsibility to work under divine direction.

EXAMPLES OF BIBLICAL STEWARDS

Who are "biblical" stewards today? Where are they? As the picture of the steward emerges in Genesis 1 and 2, most of us realize that we have met people who fit this description, people who are energetic managers in God's image and yet go about their work with the tender touch of a gardener. Perhaps you know a Virginia farmer who combines deep devotion to the soil with use of a high-tech computer to provide food for today and fertile land for the next generation; an Illinois nurse who has returned to graduate school so that she can more effectively provide health care for the poor, either here in North America or perhaps somewhere in Central America; an Indiana businessman who passed up a promotion to continue as director of the personnel office working on behalf of an ethnically diverse work force; an Ohio college janitor who watches from behind his broom for students who are lonely, inviting them out to his small farm for a visit.

Similarly we have met stewards who are not biblical in their stewardship, who work out of either Genesis 1 or 2 but not both: one physician whose medical judgment everyone trusts, but whose touch is cold; another doctor whose manner warms the spirit, but whose skill seems suspect; a philanthropist who gives generously but is arrogant and proud; a pastor who can never find time to pull together an effective sermon because individual members of the congregation need constant care and attention.

Of course, none of us can perfectly embody the biblical steward in its fullest sense. But it is important that we remember both aspects of the steward — the manager and the servant — as we work together as biblical stewards, participating in the body of Christ. Effective management and tender touch under the guidance of God — both are crucial dimensions of the steward metaphor in the biblical tradition.

POTENTIAL PROBLEMS OF THE STEWARD METAPHOR

The biblical image of the steward has the power to capture the imagination and to direct our steps. We have the God-given potential to be both effective administrators and tender gardeners, and we genuinely want to live as stewards in the image of God.

But while we affirm the value and power of the steward metaphor, we must also be aware of its potential dangers and problems. A metaphor may be appropriate and valuable in one context but not as appropriate in another. In addition, a word may have troubling connotations which our attraction to the word may tempt us to ignore. Any word with the power to engage and direct the human spirit can be dangerous. Therefore we will now turn to an examination of some concerns that have been raised in connection with this metaphor of the steward.

Outside Our Context

In a dialogue videotaped a few years ago, Douglas Hall and James Forbes touch on one potential problem with the metaphor of the steward. In this conversation Douglas Hall raises the possibility that the metaphor of the steward might not be the most helpful image for certain Christians — namely, those in what we often call the "third world." He suggests that they may want and need a more aggressive metaphor, perhaps one with a more clearly liberating ring to it.

In response, we may find ourselves agreeing with James Forbes. He insists on the radical, even revolutionary power of the steward image. This metaphor directly challenges a world where domination and oppression characterize the social and political arenas, where one group's abundance causes scarcity for another.

James Forbes is right in affirming the radical power of the steward image. Knowing that we are made in God's image with the responsibility to tend God's garden and administer God's world, we are angry when we see what the human community has done with that mandate. We want to cry out, "The problem is not the word 'steward,' but the scarcity of responsible stewards!" However, *steward* is a "managerial" word. The abuse of managerial responsibility in North America may still require third-world Christians to search for an alternative image.

Hierarchy

Others have raised questions about the value of the metaphor of steward. During a symposium at the American Academy of Religion in 1987, David Tracy asked: "Is steward really the best we can do?" His concern involved the hierarchy inherent in the word "steward": God — humanity — world. He insisted that for now we should give preference to metaphors that elicit more egalitarian pictures.

As with many of the biblical metaphors that have captured our imagination, the metaphor of steward comes from a hierarchical understanding of social relationships. As both the Joseph story and the parables of Jesus illustrate, a steward was one who implemented the policies and cared for the property of a master. By using that image from a hierarchical social structure to envision the God-human/human-world relationship, we may be writing "hierarchy" on the human spirit. Working out of a hierarchical understanding may undermine responsible stewardship.

Obviously the problem exists not only with the steward metaphor but also with other metaphors for the God-human relationship, such as master/servant and king/subject. Sallie McFague insists in her book entitled *Models of God* that we must find nonhierarchical, inclusive, destabilizing metaphors out of which to live as Christians.

21

While "steward" may be inclusive and — as James Forbes insists — destabilizing, it is certainly not nonhierarchical.

Does it really make a difference? As we have said before, the words and images that we use have a powerful effect on how we think, act, and even hope. For example, it makes an enormous difference if we image the Palestinians as refugees or as terrorists. The language we use does make a difference. The power of language to affect how we see and treat others makes us reluctant to use many labels and metaphors — for example, "retarded," "undeveloped," and "primitive."

If we use only hierarchical metaphors to image the relationship between God and humanity and between humanity and the world, it will affect how we organize our institutions and orient our action. Laypeople will continue to consider a church agency as a hierarchical power regardless of how the folks in that organization want to conceive of their work. Christians will continue to image God as a benevolent dictator living in a heavenly realm regardless of how irrelevant or unhelpful that image might be.

A related aspect of "steward" with a potential for misuse is that the metaphor may allow people to consider themselves as the most important or perhaps the only important element in God's world. Humans matter most. We rank above the animals and all other nonhuman life in the hierarchy. Therefore all other aspects of the world can be treated as secondary to our health, wealth, and happiness. In such a human-centered approach, managing for the common good means for the common human good. Tending creation's garden means ensuring the comfort of the human inhabitants. Valuing life refers first of all to human life; nonhuman life has only secondary value, and the inanimate elements of the world — soil, water, rocks, etc. — have no value except in that they support human life. Clearly, such an anthropocentric view is a distortion of our true stewardship role. This misuse of the steward metaphor is especially dangerous because such a view can lead to behavior that is destructive to the non-human world around us.

✳   ✳   ✳

The steward metaphor provides an engaging and energetic way to image the human role in the world, giving us a concrete picture of our role as managers and gardeners in God's world. It challenges us to act as stewards in the image of God, to tend God's creation effectively and with tender care. But the power of that image must not cause us to ignore its problematic aspects, especially its implications of hierarchy. We must resist our tendency to see nature as existing only for our use. We do not want to create a system in which a rock is valued only if people think it is pretty or if it contains a mineral we need. However urgently we insist that nature is our friend, or that the poor are our sisters and brothers, or that God is our co-worker, our metaphors may cause us to act otherwise.

Must we give up the image of the steward? Not at all. But we must be aware of its potential problems. Perhaps we will need to "mix our metaphors," using other images in addition to the image of the steward so as to qualify and balance it. At least we must not use the image of the steward naively. It has too much power. We can hope that since "steward" is a newly rediscovered metaphor in our world we will be able to shape it and flesh it out so as to reduce its original hierarchical tendency. However, as the secular use of this metaphor increases — by scientists and

23

economists, for example — it becomes less ours to shape. In any case the image of the steward comes to us as one way to image the relationship between God, humanity, and the world. It is available to us with all its power and problems. We must handle it with care.

Questions for Discussion and Reflection

1. A Christian steward blends effective management with tender service. Such a steward works under divine direction, empowered to exercise her or his own judgment. Who comes to mind when you think of a good steward?

2. In Genesis 1 God pronounces each element of creation "good." Is it possible to value the animal and inanimate elements in the world as highly as the human? Can you imagine ways in which that would affect regional planning and individual decision making?

3. John 3:16 begins: "For God so loved the world . . ." We usually read this verse as "God so loved *people*." Suppose John 3:16 means what it says, "world." How would we reallocate the church budget if we were to express God's care for the world — not just the people in the world?

4. List areas where you personally or the church body act as a steward in the image of God. Where has your stewardship been less admirable?

3. Disobedience and Rivalry: Genesis 3 and 4

In Genesis 1 and 2, words and actions of God commission and empower the biblical steward. As stewards, we have been entrusted with the authority and responsibility to care for human and nonhuman life and the earth on which we all live. This empowerment gives humankind a distinctive role in the ongoing drama of God's world. But this does not mean that the earth revolves around us; rather, it means that we are to assist all life, as we find opportunity, so that the ongoing history of the earth reinforces God's pronouncement: "Behold, it is very good." To say it another way, the earth is not here to support our life only, but we are here to enhance all life on earth.

The church, at its best, has taught its children to be such stewards in God's world. Typically, stewardship education begins with the children's first notions that they can "do things to help others." As children most of us received an "allowance." We could hardly wait to buy an ice cream cone or a toy we just had to have. In addition many of us can recall using part of that allowance to collect money in Sunday school to send a goat to a child who had little milk or a blanket to one threatened by the cold.

25

Perhaps you can recall when you first began to realize that such care must extend beyond people — both friends who are near and unnamed folk far away — to include the earth that sustains human life and the animals that share this earth with us.

For those of you who grew up on a farm that awareness of the need to care for the earth may always have been part of your understanding, whether or not you called it stewardship. Those of us who grew up in the city may remember camp as one place where we became conscious that dirt was not just something we were to keep out of the house, but it was also soil, absolutely central to all life on earth.

Those memories are important, and together they generate the corporate story of Christians seeking to be faithful stewards. We must ensure that our stewardship programs continue to provide young and/or new Christians the opportunity to realize the trust God has placed in them as stewards of life and the earth.

Having explored the empowering of the stewards in Genesis 1 and 2, we shall now turn to another group of texts and another chapter in the drama of human stewardship. Just as we may fondly recall our youthful and adult efforts to be God's faithful stewards, we are equally aware of our unfaithful stewardship.

The next chapters in Genesis, chapters 3–11, tell a painful story about stewards who misuse their trust. These are not happy stories, but narratives of transgression and violation by God's appointed stewards. They show humanity assuming the steward's power and acting not to care for others but to exploit, violate, and destroy. The narratives show God on the defensive — indeed, in tears (according to Genesis 6) — trying to deal with the devastation and distortion created by human unfaithfulness. Perhaps we wish these chapters were not there, or we want to dismiss them as problems of the distant past. But we cannot. No matter how reluctant we are to admit it, they bear a striking resemblance to current stories of unfaithful stewardship.

STEWARDSHIP AND SIN

The news media in North America has discovered that people do care about stewardship. Scarcely a newsmagazine or a daily paper arrives without at least one item that we recognize as a story of unfaithful stewardship. Most popular are stories involving misuse of the earth's resources: oil that darkens the beaches, chemicals that pollute the water, rain that eats the trees, gases that destroy the atmosphere.

We can rejoice that people professing no particular religious faith have joined with Christians to awaken all of us to the ever-increasing threats to the earth. Indeed, to many it seems more likely that life on earth will end in a pool of pollution than from a radioactive cloud. However, for Christians these matters are not just an issue of human survival; they are also theological issues. The problem of poor stewardship arises not just from ignorance or short-sightedness — the problem is sin. The Bible knew about sinful stewardship long before it made the evening news.

To better understand the problem of bad stewardship we can turn to the Bible's old sagas of disobedience and sin in God's world. These narratives of transgression and violation speak in story form about the mess humankind has made of its stewardship mandate. Nor can these transgression narratives be reduced to a tragedy that happened in the past, leaving us a messed-up world. They narrate the ongoing drama of life and death, forming a collage of all that humankind has done and continues to do as stewards in God's world.

We find five transgression narratives following Genesis 1 and 2. The best known are the tale of the man and woman in the garden (Gen. 3), the tale of Cain and Abel (Gen. 4), and the tale of the Tower of Babel (Gen. 11:1-9). The less well known include an anecdote about the sons of God and the daughters of humanity (Gen. 6:1-4) and a narrative concerning the violation of Noah by his son (Gen. 9:20-27). In addition to similarities in general structure and genre, each of these narratives anguishes over a natural tension that arises as humankind endeavors to live as stewards. In this chapter we will look at the narrative of the garden and the tale of two brothers.

Genesis 3

Through his typology of the first and second Adam, Paul has made Genesis 3 the most popular of these transgression stories in the Christian tradition. The tale is centered in a very familiar tension of life, the tension between freedom and limits.

As this tale begins, God has already given humanity freedom: "You may freely eat of every tree in the garden." The characters know this freedom exists because they have one identifiable and transgressable limit — namely, the tree whose fruit they must not eat. It is not hard to understand why freedom requires such a "tree." If there were no such limit, all actions that were possible would also be permitted. No freedom would exist because all choice has been eliminated. We might illustrate the lack of freedom in that situation by imagining a child setting out on an adventure through the house. If all the things in the room that could cause trouble were put out of reach, is the child free? No. All choice has been removed. The child is genuinely free only if she has the power and possibility to play with some items that are not permitted as well as those that are permitted.

Obviously freedom can be defined and described in different ways. In this narrative, freedom involves the power to choose in a world where some things are beneficial and others are harmful. This freedom to choose can be truly exercised only when limits are identifiable and transgressable. Hence genuine freedom does exist in this tale. Naturally that freedom requires discernment, followed by decision. The tension created in this decision-making process is spelled out in the conversation between the woman and the serpent: What about the tree in the garden identified as harmful — the tree we are not supposed to use for food? How can we know that we will be harmed by eating from that tree? Is the limit imposed for our benefit or perhaps for God's?

Rather than enjoying all that God has permitted, humankind has suddenly become preoccupied with the limitation, a limitation that does not appear to benefit humanity. So the woman and man take charge as they have been empowered to do. Unfortunately they choose to act as stewards in a way that leads to death rather than to life.

We usually understand this familiar story as a narrative about individual sin or collective Fall, but it is also part of the ongoing story of the steward. Living responsibly in the tension between freedom and limits is at the very heart of stewardship.

Free at Last We really have been set free in the world, God's magnificent garden. We enjoy the green, flower-dotted hills of springtime in Maryland. We see people of all shapes, sizes, ages, and colors every day on the rapid transit trains in Chicago. We listen to the birds of New Brunswick sing to their sisters and brothers in Maine. We see the wheat glow in the sunlight of Manitoba and watch

29

the ocean wash the California shore. We live in a magnificent garden.

While virtually all things are possible in God's garden, not all things are beneficial, and some things are not permitted. Nevertheless, we are genuinely free. We have the power to drain the farm soil of all its nutrients, to enslave certain people by economic oppression or military might, to care for only our own physical needs or emotional desires. We can even preach the gospel as benefiting and blessing us and condemning those not like us. But such things are not permitted for those entrusted with the stewardship of God's world; they constitute stewardship toward death in a world of life.

Yet, like the man and woman in the garden, we wonder whether the limits are really needed and beneficial for us and the planet. Often we decide to do what is not permitted — and we live with the results. The wild flowers of Maryland are buried beneath trash thrown from the cars that speed past too fast for the occupants to notice what they have done. Some of the people on the Chicago trains remain there to sleep, having no other option. Some birds of New Brunswick lay eggs too fragile to survive. The soil of Manitoba blows into Ontario, steadily reducing fertility. The ocean off California is contaminated with oil and other pollutants — products of human activity.

It is not an easy matter being God's stewards, living in a garden where so much more is possible than is beneficial. The process of discerning what is most beneficial, and to whom, consumes our time and depletes our energy. Unlike the situation in Genesis 3 where the snake actively participated in the discussion, for the most part the voice of nature has been silenced. As a result, the value of the nonhuman world has been disregarded or at the least ignored as the stewards enhance life only for themselves rather than for all of God's world.

In the tale of Genesis 3, God places a curse on nature because of the disobedience and transgression of God's limits, a transgression which affected all aspects of creation (3:14-19). In the course of the biblical narrative, God lifts this curse and promises never to reimpose it (8:21). However, by silencing nature, humankind seems to have reimposed the curse God lifted. Soil has been treated as if it were only dirt, air has been drained of its oxygen, vegetation has been valued only as harvest, and animals have been valued only as sources of food, clothing, and human companionship.

In the past and the present God's stewards have made decisions creating toxic violence in the environment and agonizing pain in the center of human life. This will almost certainly continue in the future. Disobedience based on what looks good to the human eye or is available for easy consumption will continue to bring divine judgment. Nevertheless, we can rejoice that the voice of nature is again being heard in the land. The stewards are finding new ways to nurture the soil back to life. Many stewards are reclaiming their life-enhancing role. Rather than using the streams as trash cans and diverting the water to disappear in the desert, the stewards are listening to nature's voice and deciding to let the rivers run.

Genesis 4

A second transgression narrative, Genesis 4, features rivalry in the family of stewards. As we know, the stewards of God's world have been assigned different tasks. In this narrative some till the fields and others tend the flocks. Almost inevitably tension arises among the stewards. In this tale of two brothers rivalry flares up because the fruit of one steward's labor is rewarded over that of another. Neither the narrator nor the characters tell us the reason for this preferential treatment. Scholars and lay readers alike have proposed reasons for God's decision to choose Abel's gift. However, in the end we cannot know, and apparently it is not necessary to know in order to understand the narrative.

Quite naturally, Cain, whose effort was rejected, becomes upset, even enraged. He acts to eliminate the tension by destroying his rival. The nonhuman world is affected by this violent end to the rivalry. The ground turns red in response to this violation and the blood cries out to God. With anguished inquiry — "Where is your brother?" — God enters the drama, dispensing a mixture of justice and mercy. The drama of life goes on, but it is heavily marked by alienation: alienation between person and God, between humankind and the nonhuman world, and within the human community itself.

Rivalry and Destruction   The emergence of rivalry among the community of managers and caretakers continues to plague us. Unfortunately, the destructive resolution of such rivalry often repeats itself.

Such destructive responses to rivalry ruin stewardship. We need not be unusually perceptive to notice the unfaithful stewardship arising from current rivalry between nations. We read much about people victimized by international rivalry. We hear less often about the destructive results of such rivalry on the nonhuman world. One of the most difficult stewardship tasks for Americans involves keeping the U.S. Department of Defense accountable to the environment, and the same problem exists in other countries as well. When rivalry between nations or within a nation breaks out in violence, faithful stewardship is buried alongside the spent uranium and is fouled by the spilled chemicals.

International rivalry is not the only kind that turns people into destructive stewards. Economic rivalry has reduced some to poverty in certain communities so as to provide plenty for others. International business has treated its "workers" in much the same way as human beings have treated the nonhuman world. A worker tends to be valued only insofar as she or he enhances the value of the corporation. Those who are no longer useful to the corporation are disposable. We are left with piles of discarded people alongside the heaps of junk plastic.

Rivalry rooted in religion can be even more devastating. The "others," those different from us, are not only devalued; they are despised, even demonized. Destruction of another becomes not simply an action to resolve a rivalry or redress a grievance, but a religious mandate. Rivals insist that God now looks at creation and declares: "Behold, these particular children are good and everyone else is evil. They must either be converted or destroyed." Generations are stamped almost indelibly with a theology that exterminates rivals as a matter of religious conviction.

God's Tears   God's response to such violation and destruction brings us to the centerpiece of this saga, Genesis 6–9. God looks over the earth — the people, the animals, the soil, the rivers — and "the earth was corrupt in God's sight, and the earth was filled with violence" (6:11). The sight of it struck pain in the very heart of God, bringing tears to the divine eyes.

What should be done? Perhaps it would be best to destroy everything and start over. God almost takes that route. But for reasons mostly unexpressed, God remembers Noah and the animals with him (8:1) and stops short of complete destruction. God makes a covenant with the stewards promising never again to deal with unfaithful stewardship in that way (9:9-17). God designates the rain-

33

bow as a reminder to God of that promise. However God chooses to deal with unfaithful stewardship in the future, it will not be through divinely sponsored annihilation.

Stewardship of the Globe   Obviously rivalry continues to turn stewards into merchants of death. However, that is only part of what we can observe in the human community. In response to God's commitment to continue life on earth, countless individuals and groups are reclaiming their commission as faithful stewards. For example, as stewards of reconciliation they are seeking to engage in dialogue with others — dialogue that was missing between Cain and Abel. Perhaps the story need not end in bloodshed.

We can celebrate the faithful stewardship of those who find ways for individuals and groups to channel international rivalry into creative cooperation. Both identification of poor stewardship and proposals for solutions have benefited by such cooperation. Cooperation on projects between international rivals has probably been most visible in medical research. However, even here feuding over fame and national self-interest can delay or deny care to some who need it.

International cooperation has at least retarded the destruction of some parts of the nonhuman world, such as whales, dolphins, and elephants. Attempts to overcome rivalry on other environmental issues, such as clean air and fresh water, have been somewhat less successful. Even yet, faithful stewardship of the earth is being prevented by what we must assume is the self-interest of some rivals.

In the matter of human violence against rival humans, we still have a long way to go. In only a few places have we been able to redirect rivalry when it is grounded in or supported by religion. Sometimes even in the instances of religious cooperation that have been achieved, the result appears to be only a veneer of tolerance waiting to erupt in another holocaust. We seem to find only two options — religion devoid of passion or religion devoid of rivals. To allow others to be different seems to deny the truth we ourselves affirm. But faithful stewardship demands that we find some way beyond that theological dead end.

Perhaps the most dangerous road ahead involves the process of genetic engineering. That fruit looks good to eat; it promises to assist us in providing food and curing disease. Undoubtedly some genetic creativity has been given to us as part of the garden trees from which we may freely eat. But a major question looms unanswered. At what point down the road of genetic engineering will we be faced with the tree from which we must not eat lest we completely destroy even the troubled garden in which we now live? We tend to evaluate the fruit only in terms of its value to human life — indeed, often only in terms of the lives of certain humans. How can we venture into the field of genetic engineering and remain faithful stewards of the whole globe, perhaps even beyond this globe?

God still entrusts humankind with the responsibility to manage and care for the life of the earth, in spite of the continual failure of his appointed stewards. Obviously this unfaithful stewardship continues to violate the earth, producing pain in heaven as it does on earth. Our hope lies in the fact that faithful stewardship continues to happen and to make a difference.

Questions for Discussion and Reflection

1. What example of unfaithful stewardship, arising from what you would consider "eating forbidden fruit," most concerns you?

2. What example of unfaithful stewardship arising from rivalry most concerns you, including rivalry between persons, ethnic groups, corporations, nations, and religions?

3. Can you imagine or have you seen ways beyond the destructive direction of such stewardship? For example:

a. How can we avoid misusing our knowledge while still nurturing God's gifts of wonder, exploration, and invention?

b. How can we support the passion of our particular religious truth and at the same time appreciate and learn from the global varieties of religious experience?

4. Status, Exploitation, and Protectionism: Genesis 6–11

In the previous chapter we looked at unfaithful steward-ship arising from the misuse of freedom and from rivalry in the human community. Still more of the ancient tales in Genesis warn stewards of other tensions in life that provide possibilities for destructive stewardship. Acquisition of status, situations of vulnerability, and desire for self-protection all present moments of danger that can undermine efforts to act responsibly as stewards of the earth and its inhabitants.

GENESIS 6:1-4

Seldom do we read the short tale in Genesis 6:1-4. Those who do read these few verses often shake their heads in bewilderment and hurry on to the next passage. The puzzling character of the anecdote concerning the sons of God and the daughters of humanity creates confusion for scholar as well as lay reader. It reads like an odd fragment of ancient lore. That may in fact be the case. Nevertheless we should not read over it too quickly. This enigmatic little narrative nudges us to consider the sinful stewardship that can result from the problems of status and power.

In this account it is not freedom and limits (Gen. 3) nor family rivalry (Gen. 4) but sexual attraction that generates the tension in life's drama. The attraction of the sons of God to the daughters of humanity caused them to transgress the boundary between the divine and human worlds and to seize whatever women they wanted.

This abusive invasion of the human realm created a dangerous situation. The action of the sons of God threatened to create two classes of people on earth, regular folks and semi-divine super-people. God intervened to prevent that. All earth's creatures would be mortal, living for a time and then dying in due course. To use a modern-day analogy, when we watch world-class athletes in action, we can sometimes feel that they are different from the rest of us, almost a different species of being, but this is not so. God has declared that there is only one class of human beings. No one can claim to be more.

The transgression of the divine/human boundary in this anecdote reminds us of how easy it is to forget that all people have been endowed with the image of God. The spirit of God abides in everyone, just as death comes to all. The managerial mandate has not been given to one group of giants; no one group can claim a God-given right to be in charge, while other "lesser" beings have little or no control over life.

First- and Second-Class Stewards

The biblical narratives do not assume a bland egalitarianism, but this story warns against transforming categories such as manager and worker, clergy and laity, brilliant and slow — classifications that may be functionally appropriate or even descriptively helpful at times — into natural order or divine right.

The U.S. Constitution is in many respects a most remarkable document. But Americans still suffer from a couple of decisions made at that 1787 Convention. Two groups, women and African Americans, were not enfranchised as full or "first-class" citizens. Subsequent "amendments" have tried to erase those classifications. But it is hard to remove from the collective memory the social and political "order" that these ancestors imprinted upon the American soul.

Both U.S. and Canadian citizens struggle to overcome the fact that the native "Indians" were labeled "savages." "Savage" as a noun creates a lesser, perhaps even a subhuman species. Hopefully, no one would use that noun when referring to such native citizens today. Yet the aura created by that label persists, fostered perhaps by the preferences in hair style and dress of the majority community and the feelings generated when we see native citizens dressed in their traditional style.

We are all stewards together — the rich and the famous, the poor and the nameless, the brilliant scientist and the kindergarten child, the learning disabled and the centenarian. Hence God's stewards seek to identify different stewardship roles without attaching value to one so that it demeans another.

The apostle Paul used the metaphor of the parts of the body to illustrate the critical value of different roles (1 Cor. 12). Apparently he knew that values can be attached to roles, creating the kind of status that undermines the work of the whole (1 Cor. 12:21-25). Paul observed that when values begin to elevate the status of some at the expense of others, God intervenes to honor the "inferior member" (12:24), an intervention not dissimilar to God's intervention to prevent a super-race from arising out of the actions of the sons of God (Gen. 6:3). God did not create stewards and non-stewards, nor even first- and second-class stewards.

GENESIS 9:20-27

In Genesis 9 we find another story that we frequently read past quickly, usually skipping on to the tale of the Tower of Babel. Nevertheless this tale too raises concerns that affect faithful stewardship.

Noah, a man of the soil, tended his vineyard. One harvest time he drank so much of his produce that it acted as a sedative. We need to recall that drunkenness in the ancient Near East was not an occasion for either comedy or condemnation as it is in our culture. Drinking too much wine made the drinker vulnerable to exploitation. And so it happened to Noah. Ham, one of his very own sons, exploited his father's wine-induced vulnerability.

The narrative does not tell us what Ham did, except that he "saw" the vulnerability of his father and "told" others. Many assume that Ham's transgression involved sexual abuse. Perhaps, but ancient Near Eastern texts tell us that it was the duty of a son to help his father when alcohol, age, etc., had made him vulnerable. In this tale Ham saw the vulnerability of his father but did not help him. Instead, he told others outside. His brothers, on the other hand, did assist their father. A very carefully worded sentence describes the steps the brothers took to care for their vulnerable father (9:23).

Exploitation of Vulnerability

Most of us know firsthand the temptation of the stewards to exploit the vulnerability of other people, of the animal world, and of the land. We have been either the exploiter or the exploited — often we have been both. Increasingly we have had to confront our exploitation of the inanimate inhabitants of the earth. The earth's silence makes it vulnerable. The ground that feeds us lies quiet. As we walk on the grass, the earth feels like a sleeping giant, a friendly giant. The most frequent sounds from the inanimate world include the sounds of running water and the sound of the wind as it swishes through the trees. The air, soil, and water cannot protest when we dump chemicals into streams and rivers, when we bury harmful waste, when we fill the air with toxic fumes. We exploit nature's silent vulnerability.

Ham did not pay the price for his exploitation of his father. The consequences of his actions fell on his son, Canaan. In the same way, our children and grandchildren may suffer the consequences of what we have done. They may be forced finally to listen to the silent cry of the soil and water that we chose to ignore. By that time the cry of nature may be: "Cursed be you. Exploitation by your ancestors has brought our curse upon you."

It is not only inanimate nature that stretches out before us, vulnerable to our exploitation. Many creatures in the animate world, both human and animal, find themselves exposed to such exploitation. We can anticipate that wherever vulnerability exists, some unfaithful steward will attempt to exploit it. It seems unfair that one generation of unfaithful stewards can exploit, forcing the next generation to pay for their sin. But stewardship affects not only the age we live in but the next age as well.

41

GENESIS 11:1-9

The final narrative in this trilogy is the well-known tale of the Tower of Babel. Historically the church has treated this as a story about the sin of pride. Pride clearly tarnishes the drama as the unnamed citizens sought to "make a name" for themselves. However, another concern motivated the "builders" as well, one that appears every bit as dangerous and perhaps more insidious than the sin of pride.

The community decided to build the tower because of fear, fear of being scattered: "Let us build ourselves a city . . . otherwise we shall be scattered abroad upon the face of the whole earth" (11:4). Their fear sounds familiar: "We shall be separated from our family, our loved ones." "We shall lose our way of life." The fear of losing their "home" acted as a very powerful catalyst as they built a city and tower to protect what they had.

The citizens of "Babel" built their protection. However, divinely inspired "irony" overturned their efforts. The very device designed to protect their community proved to be the cause of their undoing: "The LORD came down to see the city and the tower, which mortals had built. . . . So the LORD scattered them abroad from there . . ." (Gen. 11:5, 8).

Protectionism

The urge of self-protection seems to be a common problem among stewards. The unfaithful steward in Jesus' parable sought to protect what he had been given by burying it in the ground (Matt. 25:14-30). He might have built a huge building around it to be even more sure of its protection.

Thrifty Christians seem especially susceptible to protectionist stewardship. We spend an enormous amount of our money and energy to protect ourselves, our family, our way of life. The insurance industry would encourage us to spend even more.

Our love for family, church, and country very often leads us to turn our energy to building in order to protect them — "lest we be scattered abroad upon the face of the whole earth." It may be easiest to see dangerous protectionism in the nuclear shield we have built around us. The shield grows thicker and higher, now reaching into outer space. And still we fear being scattered, our community destroyed. Even if the relaxation of some international tensions allows us to "drop our guard" slightly, danger emerges in some new place. This generates another flurry of protectionist activity designed to "protect our self-interests," as presidents of the United States frequently declare.

Our protectionism appears as often in economic as in military activity. We seek to protect our standard of living from being scattered to the poor corners of the globe. So we subsidize agricultural commodities and place tariffs on manufactured goods. In so doing we hope to protect our farmers and our industry. But often irony invades our planned protection as it did at "Babel" in the ancient tale. The agricultural subsidies intended to protect our farmers increase the income of the huge agri-business corporations, thus undermining the small farmer. Tariffs designed to protect the small business instead support the greedy corporations that buy up the small entrepreneurs, closing or moving the factory to wherever conditions favor the corporation.

Church and Home

What happens in business and in the military may differ only in scope compared to what also occurs in the church and the family. At a given time each year, almost every congregation meets to decide how it will spend its anticipated income. At that point those gathered in conversation seek to identify the line between appropriate nurture of the local congregation and self-destructive protection of the "home" community. Opinions differ — usually energetically, sometimes angrily.

The identification of the difference between a nurturing and a protectionist budget proves almost impossible to identify, especially in the abstract. Some congregational research has tried to put percentage figures on appropriate "local" and "outreach" sections of the budget. While no percentage fits all congregations or even any one congregation all of the time, budgets that are dramatically lopsided one way or the other clearly signal danger. We must confess that in most congregations the budget tends to lean in the direction of local protectionism. But there are congregations who neglect caring for their facilities and people in an effort to "make a name" for themselves in terms of their mission or service budget.

Protectionist stewardship also happens in connection with the family. Preoccupation with preserving the family as we want it often furthers its destruction and scattering. The church, in its laudatory effort to applaud the "ideal" family (unbroken marriage, well-adjusted children), often further alienates families which do not measure up. Within the family, efforts to "build a city" or "make a name for ourselves" frequently destroy the family the efforts were designed to protect. Of course, the opposite happens just as frequently. The disregard of the family in order for selected family members to build their own tower or make their own name proves equally destructive. In fact, the occasions for unfaithful stewardship in the family prove so frequent that we marvel that any families survive. But they do, by the grace of God and because of the responsible actions of many stewards.

MANY STEWARDS: 1 KINGS 19

Elijah found himself surrounded by sinful stewards seeking to destroy him, so he ran. Elijah ran as far south as he could, into the desert, away from a society that appeared to be headed for collapse because of the actions of countless sinful stewards. He ran until he came to the mountain of God. When given the opportunity, Elijah complained to God about the whole mess. In spite of all his efforts to live as a responsible steward, things had only gotten worse. As far as he could tell, he was absolutely the only faithful steward left in the land, and now the forces of destruction were seeking to kill him too (19:10).

After a long and eventful wait in which Elijah experienced wind, earthquake, fire, and finally the "sound of sheer silence" (19:12), Elijah came out of his cave and received a response from God. In effect, God called Elijah back to work. But God also reassured him that there were thousands of faithful stewards still at work in Israel (19:18). Elijah was not alone.

Elijah's world was small compared to the global society in which we live. If God found several thousand faithful stewards in Israel, how many more must be at work all around our world? We often find ourselves preoccupied with and defeated by the destructive stewardship that surrounds us. No one can deny the danger to the family, the church, human society, and nature. Nevertheless, if we were to react to this danger as Elijah did, by running as far away as possible, even to the mountain of God, we would likely receive an answer similar to the one Elijah heard: Work on and notice the faithful stewardship that is happening as far as the eye can see.

As Far as the Eye Can See

Obviously some stewards receive more public notice than others. Unfortunately that attention can be given on the basis of status rather than faithfulness. The scene of the widow who had only a "mite" but was a faithful steward with the little she had continues to be re-enacted (Mark 12:41-44). If we look closely we can find a myriad of people who, though they have just a mite of stewardship capacity, exercise it in ways that put many of us to shame. For example, those whose mental ability falls below the norm sometimes have sensitivities, especially toward nature, that highly rational and intelligent individuals lack. Those whose age has drained much of their energy can often provide wise counsel that youth cannot match. Those who, because of accident or illness, cannot work fast often learn patience and discipline that the more able-bodied lack. Belatedly perhaps, but increasingly, the community of faith is discovering new truth in the affirmation that all have been created in the image of God and endowed by their Creator with steward-ship responsibility. The spirit of God does not abide in some completely and in others only a little.

Almost everyone agrees that those less strong should never be abused and those less able should not be exploited. Yet such exploitation happens frequently — and not just at the hands of those whom we recognize as mean-spirited and violent. Our voting preferences create a web of poverty from which only a few poor can escape. Mental and physical handicaps elicit laughter or indifference from most of us and help from only a few. And yet there are signs of change.

We can only be amazed at the speed with which North Americans are adjusting our lifestyle to enrich the soil, when we have been used to dumping on the earth for so long. Much remains to be done to care for the soil, the air, and the water. Admittedly many times we only act when the problems of the animal and inanimate world threaten human life and welfare. But occasionally we respond carefully because we see that the earth lies before us as vulnerable to human exploitation as drunken Noah. Acting to support and enrich the earth and everything in it, we not only care for the vulnerable earth but enhance life for now and the next generation.

Our response to abuse in the global family has been equally remarkable. Admittedly many times this response has been selective, directed toward exploitation nearest us. Nevertheless, because of the availability of global information, we hear about and even see abuse that not long ago could have remained hidden. Thanks to an international network of assistance agencies, we can address victimization that not long ago remained invisible.

The problem of self-destructive protection of local interests still haunts us. Yet, prompted in part by awareness of our single global economy, we realize that we have no local interests that are not affected by the well-being of the global community. While we acknowledge the many negative aspects of the Christian missionary movement of the nineteenth and twentieth centuries, it did at least have the positive effect of making North American Christians aware that we are part of a global church. The sun may eventually set on every national empire, but it cannot set on the body of Christ.

This global church membership has also made us aware that we share the globe with those who do not profess Jesus

Christ as Lord. These folk live as our neighbors at home and abroad. Part of Christian stewardship involves affirming our faith passionately while at the same time working with those who make other faith decisions. We find this road filled with rocks and unmarked turns, but as stewards of the mysteries of Christ, we are finding our way slowly. As one might expect, Christians in other parts of the globe who are in the minority in their society can lead the way for those of us who are North American Christians.

The problem of unfaithful — indeed sinful — stewardship shows no signs of disappearing. As stewards struggling to be faithful, we frequently have become so overwhelmed by sinful stewardship and unmet needs that we have been unaware of occasions when life has been enhanced by the work of faithful stewards. Amid the tragic events of sinful stewardship — including misuse of position, exploitation of vulnerability, and parochial protectionism — we can also find good and faithful stewards hard at work. Sometimes they may seem like an occasional flower in a field of thistles, but we can locate them if we look closely: those who humble themselves, taking the form of a servant, rather than exalting themselves and seizing whatever they desire; those who carefully assist the more vulnerable inhabitants of this globe, rather than exploiting whatever they can control; those who use their resources for the benefit of the earth today and tomorrow, rather than protecting only their present self-interests. God continues to say "Well done" to faithful stewards such as these on many occasions, even while being disappointed in the failures of humanity as a whole far too often.

Questions for Discussion and Reflection

1. Identify examples of the following types of sinful stewards, either from personal knowledge or from news reports:

    a. Individuals whose exercise of power or self-glorification has demeaned others, treating them as inferior stewards of God's world.

    b. Persons who have exploited the vulnerability of less powerful segments of the web of life on earth, either animate or inanimate.

    c. People whose efforts to protect their own interests have undermined the interests of other people and things.

2. Whether or not you are willing to label it divine judgment, have you seen such sinful stewardship bear sour fruit for the exploiter as well as the exploited? Can you anticipate this happening, or will the "next generation" always pay the price?

3. Identify stewards who act for the benefit of those less fortunate, less powerful, or even several generations in the future.

4. Undoubtedly antagonism experienced by Christians both at home and around the world is in some measure the result of our unfaithful stewardship of the mysteries of Christ. Have you seen the Good News turned bad by abuse of power or exploitation of vulnerability? We seem never to exhaust occasions when our prayers must feature confession.

5. Moses: Steward of God's Covenant

This generation seems to be involved in a frustrating search for heroes, women or men whose actions or character can serve as a model for others. Many find the search frustrating because just when we think we have located the perfect candidate, something goes wrong. All heroes come with a character tainted by indiscretion or success tarnished by failure.

Those of us involved in stewardship appear no less determined in our pursuit of exemplary stewards, persons about whom we can say, "Now that is what we mean by a good steward." This search is very difficult since we live in a world of stewards every bit as sinful as those described in Genesis 3–11. Contemporary figures frequently do not live up to our lofty expectations, or, even if they do set a good example of faithful stewardship, they are so utterly unique, so odd, that no garden-variety Christian could or would follow in their footsteps. And turning to the Bible often does not help, since biblical figures do not transfer easily to our world. They would not know a silicon chip from holy manna.

In spite of the risks in turning to a book not ac-

50

quainted with our modern world, we may find no more suitable hero for stewardship program and practice than Moses. Obviously Moses does not come to us without flaw or failure. Nor are we accustomed to think of Moses as a steward. In the tradition of the church and the synagogue we know Moses the liberator and Moses the lawgiver. But Moses' role as steward is just as central as any other heroic role Moses played in his time.

As with most heroes, Moses is bigger than any single title applied to him, even that of steward, but we will look at only a single facet of this biblical giant. The stories and tradition portray Moses functioning as a steward mainly in terms of his role as steward of God's covenant. The Bible displays a rich variety of covenantal perspectives. We will explore one that is primarily, though not exclusively, tied to Moses. This Mosaic form of covenant features the careful connection between gift and responsibility. We will see that this "gift and responsibility" covenant tradition forms the central theology of stewardship as we have customarily defined it.

COVENANTAL CONFUSION

But first a short "aside" about covenant in the Bible. Contrary to what we might wish, the Bible does not explain covenant to us very well. Through careful study of covenant in ancient Israel and the Hebrew Bible, scholars have managed to discern some of the variety of ways in which the Bible uses the word *covenant*. But the Bible does not sit us down and say, "Now I want to explain covenant to you." The word *covenant* will continue to be a matter of scholarly discussion, if not dispute, far beyond our time — but at least this lack of clarity will provide work for biblical scholars who might otherwise end up unemployed.

The Bible does not define covenant with an encyclopedic article, as we might prefer. Rather than including a page or even a sentence defining covenant, the Bible tells stories that embody covenant. It is similar to the time when Jesus was asked to define "neighbor." Rather than saying, "Listen up, let me explain the concept 'neighbor' to you," Jesus said, "Let me tell you a story," and he told the story we know as the parable of the good Samaritan (Luke 10:29-37).

THE STORY OF MOSES

It appears that when the ancient storytellers set about telling the story of Moses, they saw "covenant" as the dominant theme of his life story. Hence, as we listen to the story of Moses, we find not only a person who believed in covenant or talked about covenant or even participated in covenant, but one whose life pilgrimage was essentially the story of covenant.

The tale told by the storytellers in ancient Israel described a baby boy born into a family of an oppressed people who were living as foreigners in a land which was not their home. By law this boy's life should have ended at birth. Surprisingly, that did not happen. A group of women, mostly unnamed, surreptitiously defied the law and through intrigue and ingenuity saved this boy's life. These women — a midwife, a mother, a sister, and a royal daughter — conspired to save at least one Hebrew baby boy. It is a magnificent story of risk and danger.

Hence the beginning of life for Moses came as a gift through cunning and courageous women who, according to the narrator, feared God. All infants receive the gift of life through birth, but Moses got more than most. He was gifted with life not once but twice, and in addition he was given a home — apparently a royal home — food and love, both a wet nurse and a parent. To refresh your memory, here is a short excerpt from the story:

> Then [Moses'] sister said to Pharaoh's daughter, "Shall I go and call you a nurse from the Hebrew women to nurse the child for you?" And Pharaoh's daughter said to her, "Go." So the girl went and called the child's mother. . . . And the child grew, and she brought him to Pharaoh's daughter, and he became her son. (Exod. 2:7-10, RSV)

In the Mosaic tradition, covenant always begins with gift. Moses received from these women a gift, an inheritance: life, home, and sustenance. But the story does not end there; it moves from gift to responsibility. The gifted one is responsible to use those gifts for others. So we are not surprised when, in the second chapter of the story, Moses encounters God on a sacred mountain and receives his instructions for how he must live responsibly. This gifted one, Moses, has been called by God to help others: "Come, I will send you to Pharaoh to bring my people, the Israelites, out of Egypt" (Exod. 3:10).

With a lot of help from God, and some from his brother and sister, Moses did for the whole people what the women had done for him. Admittedly Moses demonstrated more reluctance and some would say less skill than the women showed. Be that as it may, through divine power and the responsible action of a few people, the Israelites, whose future had been controlled by death, oppression, and separation, received a gift: freedom, land, and a life-sustaining covenant with God. In order that the Israelites would always remember their giftedness, they were taught to recite this brief account of their covenantal story:

A wandering Aramean was my ancestor; he went down into Egypt and lived there as an alien, few in number, and there he became a great nation, mighty and populous. When the Egyptians treated us harshly and afflicted us, by imposing hard labor on us, we cried to the LORD, the God of our ancestors; the LORD heard our voice and saw our affliction, our toil, and our oppression. The LORD brought us out of Egypt with a mighty hand and an outstretched arm . . . and he brought us into this place and gave us this land, a land flowing with milk and honey. (Deut. 26:5-9)

FROM GIFT TO RESPONSIBILITY

Just as in Moses' story, Israel's covenantal story begins with gift and moves to responsibility. Like Moses, the Israelites have an encounter with Yahweh, again at a sacred mountain, in which they are given instructions for fulfilling their covenantal responsibilities. Listen to Moses reminding later generations of this meeting:

Hear, O Israel, the statutes and ordinances that I am addressing to you today; you shall learn them and observe them diligently. The LORD our God made a covenant with us at Horeb. Not with our ancestors did the LORD make this covenant, but with us, who are all of us here alive today. The LORD spoke with you face to face at the mountain, out of the fire. (Deut. 5:1-4)

Because the Israelites had received gifts from God, they also had the responsibility of observing God's statutes and ordinances. These rules or laws had nothing to do with legalism as we normally think about it — that is, as a heavy burden of strict laws established to control and dominate. God's statutes and ordinances are guidelines for living out the responsibility that follows from God's gracious gift.

CONCERNING PAUL

Our reading of Paul, which traditionally emphasizes unconditional gift, has done us an immense disservice concerning covenant. By emphasizing what Paul says about gift without paying attention to the complementary idea of responsibility, we have misunderstood Paul's message. In fact, there may be no one in the whole biblical tradition who understands better than Paul the "gift and responsibility" covenant tradition.

Gift and responsibility appear together many times in Paul's writings, but we will look at only one example — Paul's Letter to the Galatians. He begins with a discussion of the gifts Christians have received through Christ, especially the gifts of freedom and community:

> . . . In Christ Jesus you are all children of God through faith. As many of you as were baptized into Christ have clothed yourselves with Christ. There is no longer Jew or Greek, there is no longer slave or free, there is no longer male and female; for all of you are one in Christ Jesus. (Gal. 3:26-28)

After talking about the gifts of freedom and community in Christ, Paul uses the last part of the letter to remind them that the second dimension of covenant involves responsibility.

> For you were called to freedom, brothers and sisters; only do not use your freedom as an opportunity for self-indulgence, but through love become slaves to one another. (Gal. 5:13)

We cannot understand Paul unless we understand the relationship between gift and responsibility both in the life of Moses and in covenant.

THE THEOLOGY OF STEWARDSHIP

If any group should understand covenant in the tradition of Moses, it should be those concerned with stewardship. Mosaic covenant provides the bedrock of the most frequently used biblical theology of stewardship: gift and responsibility. Whether we are talking about stewardship of the earth, our financial resources, or the gospel, we remind people of the gifts God has given them and their responsibility to be good stewards.

Overemphasizing Responsibility

There are problems with our use of this covenant tradition. Sometimes we place too much emphasis on the last half of the story of Moses, as if his story and the story of ancient Israel began at Sinai. In other words, we emphasize the "responsibility" half of the covenant, while sometimes omitting or rushing through the "gift" part. Not that we leave out the gift dimension, but frequently it seems that we mention God's bountiful gifts only as a prelude to the important part, the responsibility. Often we don't intend to do this, but it comes through in our attitudes and the implications of what we say.

This signal came through loud and clear in a recent stewardship meeting. The gift-responsibility paradigm formed the implicit theology. The speaker earnestly reminded her listeners that in the "first world" we have been given so much more than those in the "other two-thirds," and that "to whom much has been given, much will be required." She talked about gift. But gift got swallowed up in an urgent call to responsibility. Essentially this speech was a first-world Protestant reading of the parable of the talents (Matt. 25:14-30). God has given us gifts, but primarily as a test to see if we will be responsible.

We do not fool our brothers and sisters with that kind of discussion of gift. They know the part that really counts for us is responsibility. They listen with pseudo-attention on stewardship Sunday as we talk about the gift God has given us through Jesus Christ or the gifts each person has: time, talent, money. They know the other shoe will drop, the one that we think really matters — responsibility.

In fact, not only does responsibility swallow up gift, but the joy of receiving God's gift is further eroded by guilt: we ought not to have been given so much. Guardians of responsibility constantly remind us that our abundance represents an uneven distribution of global wealth. They are correct. Injustice must always remain an urgent concern of stewards. But too much emphasis on responsibility can cause a problem in stewardship education. By sounding with shrill urgency the demand for responsible behavior, we silence the song of God's gifts, so that only the responsibility half of covenant remains audible. That results in stewardship grounded not in covenant, but in duty, demand, and guilt. Exhaustion and obligation replace energy and joy as the most prominent features of a steward's life.

Like many of us, Paul was raised in a religious tradition dominated by duty; he too grew up mostly hearing the last half of the story of Moses, the responsibility part: "I am a Jew . . . educated strictly according to our ancestoral law" (Acts 22:3). In a way Paul's education was similar to that which makes a good stewardship leader: a heavy sense of responsibility. But we must not forget that the story of Moses begins not with a command to responsible behavior, but with those unnamed subversive women who gave him life, a home, and sustenance. That is where stewardship programs must start. The next chapter will focus on the gift aspect of covenant even more directly, but for now this warning bears repeating: if we do not convey to people that covenant begins with gift, they will not listen to "the rest of the story." If we emphasize only responsibility, we are trying to sell them only half of the Mosaic covenant.

Irresponsibility

In spite of our tendency to overemphasize it, the Mosaic covenant does call us to live responsibly out of our relationship with God. If we frequently overemphasize duty, it may be in reaction to the life-style we see around us. We live in a time and culture of rampant overconsumption and wastefulness, a world where people frequently cheat or steal from others and waste or hoard what they have. It is an age sick with irresponsibility. It may not be worse than previous ages, but it is certainly bad enough.

Isn't it necessary to emphasize responsibility in such an age, when so few listen? It is a time of raging sin and evil that threatens not just a given people, but the planet itself. Do we not need a thundering prophet of responsibility like Amos to shout, "Let justice roll down like waters, and righteousness like an everflowing stream" (5:24)?

Perhaps so. The irresponsibility of our time generates deep within us cauldrons of anger and tears of frustration that rival any prophet in ancient Israel. However, one wonders if simply raising the volume will help. It may only numb the nerve endings and increase the deafness. Perhaps we must instead try offering the full Mosaic covenant, a covenant that sings and dances in celebration of what we have been given, a covenant that engages intently in conversation around the mountain of God concerning our responsibility. Even in such an age, we must resist the temptation to stress only the responsibility half of the covenant, knowing that experiencing the full Mosaic covenant — gift as well as responsibility — will get us farther in the end.

The Mosaic Model

Experiencing both parts of the Mosaic covenant does make a difference in stewardship. We will accomplish more by offering the whole Mosaic covenant and allowing responsibility to grow out of gratitude for gifts than by merely beating people over the head about responsibility.

"Jan" is an example of someone who experienced such a transformation. Jan's life in many ways could be termed uneventful. She admits that her story would not sell on the supermarket shelf unless she invented a lot of passion and trauma to add to it. There were rocky moments, more inside Jan than out, although a father who drank too much and two miscarriages before she carried a child to term caused very real hurt.

It was her ten-year college reunion that brought Jan to a new understanding of the Mosaic covenant, although she did not have the language to call it that. Seeing old friends and hearing about people she had not thought of in years gave Jan a chance to notice something she had not realized before — the many, many people who had touched her life, who had in a very real sense gifted her with life, home, and sustenance. Several of those people sat with her in that room, although many were elsewhere: her family, her teachers, a myriad of friends, and many others, both named and nameless.

That evening was not a religious conversion for Jan, but it was the beginning of one. At that time she really had no religious language, no biblical context in which to set her story. It was only later that Jan could understand the people in her life as God's gifts to her — gifts of life, home, and sustenance.

As Jan herself explained it, her sense of giftedness was the ground out of which her stewardship arose. No one had to talk to Jan about responsibility. She excitedly planned new ventures in giving to others what had been given to her. She may not have remembered much about the story of Moses, but she told about her own "stewardship" conversion in a manner very similar to the covenant model used by the storytellers in ancient Israel to narrate the story of Moses.

Jan apparently used the Mosaic paradigm accidentally, or at least unconsciously. As we seek to ground our theology of stewardship in the biblical story, we can be more intentional. If the story of Moses resonates with the reasons we give for stewardship, hopefully we will learn that story and its theology so well that we can clearly and passionately answer for the faith that is in us.

Indeed, if we want to identify a biblical stewardship hero, the story of Moses is a good one for us to learn by heart. It lays out a covenantal model for grounding stewardship that will serve us well. Stewardship begins with celebration of God's gifts. In response to God's grace, we seek to live as stewards of God's covenant.

Questions for Discussion and Reflection

1. How do you understand covenant in the Bible? Is the sequence of "gift and responsibility" familiar to you as a way to describe covenant in the biblical tradition?

2. Does the story of your life as a steward follow the "flow" of the story of Moses from gift to responsibility? Have you shared such stories of the "birth" of a steward with one another?

3. Have you been beaten over the head with responsibility until you have become numb and unable to pay attention, no matter how loud or urgent the message? What would it take to break through that numbness so that you could listen and respond?

4. How can we design our stewardship message so that the listeners experience the whole story of covenant in the tradition of Moses, gift as well as responsibility?

6. Sarah and Abraham: Stewards of God's Promise

The last chapter focused on the biblical covenant associated with Moses. As Christians concerned about stewardship, we are familiar with the Mosaic covenant. Frequently, though often unconsciously, our stewardship literature reflects such Mosaic "authorship." In this chapter we will explore a less familiar covenant tradition, one which is associated with Sarah and Abraham. This covenant tradition may seem somewhat foreign to ears accustomed to hearing the more usual theology of stewardship. In fact, some may find it more subversive than supportive. However, as we seek to ground our stewardship practice and program in the Bible, we need to push into unfamiliar territory as well as to re-examine familiar ground.

Most of us have some sense of what the Bible means by covenant, however vague that may be. In chapter five we looked at one covenant tradition, the covenant associated with Moses. That covenant combined divine gift with human responsibility, as can be seen in the opening of the Decalogue:

I am the LORD your God, who brought you out of the land of Egypt, out of the house of slavery; you shall have no other gods before me. (Exod. 20:2-3)

You may have wished that studying the Mosaic covenant would give us a workable model of covenant throughout the Bible. You may have been disappointed that the last chapter did not provide a definitive description of covenant in the Bible. Unfortunately, neither will this one. No such definitive description is possible. The biblical covenant defies such definitional control. Trying to extract a single definition drains the life out of covenant.

Therefore, any attempt to place covenant into a model or structure, including the one here, will lose some of the richness of biblical covenant. Nevertheless, we can point to some of the facets of this biblical diamond without claiming to display the whole gem. In this chapter we will look at a second covenant tradition in the Bible, one connected with such people as Noah and David as well as Sarah and Abraham. While this covenant tradition is not unrelated or antithetical to the one associated with Moses, it is distinctively different, as we will see.

DIVINE PROMISE

Divine promise is central to covenant in the tradition of Sarah and Abraham. Throughout the saga in Genesis 12 to 25 we find several speeches of divine promise to Sarah and Abraham. One speech of divine promise that takes place in the context of covenant appears in Genesis 15. After describing a mysterious night ceremony, the narrator says,

On that day the LORD made a covenant with Abram, saying, "To your descendants I give this land . . ." (Gen. 15:18)

We need not focus on the exact content of this promise in order to understand this covenant model, for the content can change, as we shall see. But the central feature of this type of covenant remains the same in every instance: the covenant is initiated by and grounded in a *divine speech of promise*. We will see promise each time.

Let's look at a second speech of divine promise, different in language and probably also in origin, but still connected with Sarah and Abraham — the covenant speech in Genesis 17. God addresses Abraham, saying,

As for me, this is my covenant with you: You shall be the ancestor of a multitude of nations. . . . I will make you exceedingly fruitful; and I will make nations of you, and kings shall come from you. I will establish my covenant between me and you, and your offspring after you throughout their generations, for an everlasting covenant, to be God to you and to your offspring after you. (17:4-7)

No single biblical character dominates the promissory covenant tradition as Moses does the gift and responsibility covenant. We can see another example of this divine promissory covenant in God's covenant with David. This divine speech of promise comes to David through Nathan:

When your days are fulfilled and you lie down with your ancestors, I will raise up your offspring after you, . . . and I will establish his kingdom. . . . Your house and your kingdom shall be made sure forever before me; your throne shall be established forever. (2 Sam. 7:12-16)

The content of this promise is different from the promises to Sarah and Abraham, but nonetheless promise remains the central feature of the covenant. If the main features of the Mosaic covenant are gift and responsibility, the central element of this covenant is promise — hence its designation as the *promissory* covenant.

UNCONDITIONAL PROMISE

This single element makes the promissory covenant distinctive in the biblical tradition. There are no conditions, no qualifications, no human responsibility connected with this covenant. It is just a promise, with no strings attached.

In this covenant God makes an unconditional promise without requiring any particular human response. Obviously the people in the narratives do respond in a variety of ways, but neither the present nor the future of the covenant depends on human activity. This characteristic makes the promissory covenant foreign or even subversive for stewardship theology and program. How can we have a stewardship program that does not focus on what we are to supposed to do as "good" stewards?

Another feature of promissory covenant makes it even more radical: God grants the covenant in perpetuity! In the examples of divine promise we looked at above and in God's covenant with Noah in Genesis 8 and 9, the words "forever," "everlasting," and "throughout all generations" appear not just once but several times. That repetition ensures that we listeners do not miss this feature. God will stand by this covenant world without end, amen. It sounds a bit like the promise at the end of Matthew's Gospel: "Lo, I am with you always, to the close of the age" (Matt. 28:20, RSV). The similarity may be more than coincidental.

The promissory covenant does not require us to be responsible stewards in order for the benefits of the covenant to happen. Responsibility is written into the covenant, but that responsibility belongs to God, not to us. God promises to be present and active in making the future happen without depending on human goodness, obedience, or faithfulness. God promises Sarah and Abraham, David, or, in the case of Noah, all humanity, to be active in bringing them life, health, and prosperity forever.

PROMISSORY COVENANT AND STEWARDSHIP

This has an unfamiliar and perhaps undesirable ring in terms of our efforts to convince or cajole people into being faithful stewards. As we discussed in the previous chapter, the customary and perhaps preferred theology for steward-ship puts its emphasis on human responsibility. Allowing for variation and nuances, the flow of the customary stewardship theology goes something like this:

1. God the Creator and Redeemer has given us life, home, and sustenance.

2. As followers of Christ, we are the primary trustees for what God has created and redeemed (i.e., re-created).

3. We are responsible to use God's gifts for the benefit of all the families of the earth, this generation and hereafter.

4. If we neglect to be good stewards we and/or our descendants will reap the negative consequences.

The Future Depends on Us?

Traditional stewardship theology, with its emphasis on our necessary action, downplays the role of God in the ongoing drama of life. It suggests that God's most decisive action occurred in the past: "The LORD brought us out of Egypt with a mighty hand . . . and gave us this land, a land flowing with milk and honey" (Deut. 26:8-9). We can see the same thing in the creation story: "In the beginning God created the heavens and the earth" (Gen. 1:1, RSV); "the LORD God formed [a human being] of dust from the ground" (Gen. 2:7, RSV). In both cases, we find the same structure. The primary locus of God's action lies in the past. The future depends on us. A well-known passage from Moses' speech in Deuteronomy puts it about as starkly as possible:

> See, I have set before you this day life and prosperity, death and adversity. If you obey the commandments of the LORD your God . . . the LORD your God will bless you in the land. . . . But if your heart turns away, . . . I declare to you today that you shall perish. . . . Choose life so that you and your descendants may live. (Deut. 30:15-19)

God will act in the future, but that future divine action will be connected with or in response to our stewardship. We will get what we deserve: that which we sow, we will also reap. Hence as stewards we determine the future of life on planet earth. Poor stewardship will destroy us — not just us personally, but the church, the earth, and perhaps beyond.

That may be overstating the case somewhat in order to point out the distinctive element in promissory covenant. Nevertheless, we need to see the different character of the unconditional divine promise of the Abrahamic (or Davidic or Noahic) covenant from the covenant theology that undergirds our traditional stewardship thinking. In virtually all stewardship literature we find an urgent appeal to accept our responsibility based on God's action through Jesus Christ on our behalf. God has acted in the past; we are accountable for what we have been given. Depending on the urgency of the moment, our stewardship literature can sound the life or death note as loudly as the passage from Deuteronomy: if we do not act as faithful stewards, we shall perish, we and our descendants.

Texts featuring God's promissory covenant are virtually unknown in our traditional stewardship theology. The texts in which God has unilaterally assumed responsibility to act on behalf of life in the future as well as in the past seem out of place. But the texts of God's promissory covenant will not disappear and they should not be ignored. We need their reminder that the future does not depend solely on our willingness to live up to our covenant responsibility. The future depends as much on God as on us; in fact, according to the promissory covenant the future depends on God *instead* of us.

The Trouble with Unconditional Promise

Certainly the theology of God's promissory covenant is familiar to us as Christians. We have all heard the Good News of God's unconditional grace. Hence we can respond to the promissory covenant by saying, "Of course. We believe that."

We affirm a theology of God's grace, but we also

want very quickly to add a "but . . ." In so doing we dilute the radical dimensions of God's promissory covenant. For several reasons, some good and some perhaps not so good, we want to reinsert human accountability quickly after announcing God's grace.

Let us start with the good reason first: We believe in justice. We grow wary whenever someone starts talking about God's beneficial action without regard to human faithfulness. We worry that God's "grace" will be cheapened to forgive all manner of human irresponsibility. The promissory covenant threatens cheap and unjust grace: we can do whatever we want, because God will take care of us and the future. It sounds like the kind of behavior that Jeremiah condemned in his day; he told the people who acted with complete disregard to fairness and justice but felt secure because they went to "church" regularly:

> Do not trust in these deceptive words: "This is the temple of the LORD, the temple of the LORD, the temple of the LORD" (Jer. 7:4)

We believe in a just God. And because God is just, in God's commonwealth what a person sows bears a clear relationship to the harvest.

Another reason for our concern about the theology of God's promissory covenant is less admirable. The affirmation that the future depends on God takes the future out of our hands, out of our control. We like to be in control, especially in our culture. Our whole life is built on control: control of production, disease, nature — control of everything. To genuinely live in God's promissory covenant not only plays near the edge of Christian irresponsibility, but also tends to undermine the foundation of North American culture. So we prefer the more traditional covenant theology for stewardship, the one in which we feel more in control.

A Broader Theology of Covenant

Nevertheless, using the covenant tradition of Moses in our stewardship theology without the covenant tradition of Sarah, Abraham, David, and Noah exposes only one facet of covenant in the Bible, giving us a partial theology of covenant. Perhaps even more important, it means that we have basically consigned God to the past. We have taken charge of the present and future, leaving God only the role of co-worker or co-creator with us. That constitutes a serious problem in traditional stewardship theology, and more and more people are noticing it.

Joanne Swenson has written an article in the October 1989 issue of *Bible Review* that deserves more than a casual reading. As assistant pastor in Boston's Old South Church, she could not understand why so many highly educated professors from Boston's eminent universities chose to attend churches that were theologically very conservative, sometimes fundamentalist — churches whose theology in important ways stood diametrically opposed to the professors' own learning and teaching. Eventually she realized that one reason could be traced to the anemic theology of the so-called liberal churches. The conservative churches preached about a God who is making things happen, a real God, a God of the present as well as the past.

There are enormous problems with the manner and scope of the presentation of God in the "conservative" churches as well, as the title of Swenson's article indicates ("Neither the Liberal nor the Conservative God Is Adequate"). Nevertheless, what she found in the so-called mainline churches was an unreal God, almost an elusive spirit. The preachers in most of these congregations refrain from saying anything confidently about God. According to Swenson, the liberal community has focused on what it could grasp, namely us — our responsibilities and prob-

70

lems, our defeats and victories. The conservative churches have never stopped talking about God — God as a real and active presence in our lives and in the world.

SHARING THE WORLD WITH GOD

Promissory covenant — that is, covenant in the tradition of Sarah and Abraham — suggests that we get used to sharing the world with God. God cannot be reduced to a spirit which moves in the human heart. God must not be assigned only or mainly the role of past creator and redeemer. Instead, God acts as a powerful presence in the events of life on earth and beyond. We need to give up the prideful proverb, "God has no hands but human hands." We must erase that nonbiblical proverb from our lived theology as well as from our confessions of faith.

Traditional creeds, confessions, and songs celebrate God's promissory covenant. Classical hymnody, insofar as it used the Psalms, features a heavy dose of God's promissory covenant. Not surprisingly, we find it in the Hebrew fourteenth-century song, "The God of Abraham Praise." We sing about God's present and future action in the traditional Welsh hymn, "Guide Me, O Thou Great Jehovah," in the more recent folk hymns from the African-American church, and in the so-called "gospel" hymns.

However, in our preaching and discussion we seem to be much more reserved. We are wary of talking about God's presence and action in the world today. We prefer to play it safe and talk only about what we know — human sin and human responsibility. The presence and action of God has been consigned to the "still small voice" in the human heart. We choose to concentrate on what we must do, as outlined in Micah 6:8:

What does the LORD require of you
but to do justice, and to love kindness,
and to walk humbly with your God?

We hesitate to expect — let alone require — any action from God in our world today. If we speak at all about God's role, we speak of God's love and care. When we are required to say what this "love and care" means, we talk about God's quiet presence in times of celebration and suffering. We are hesitant to go much farther. This may overstate our reluctance, but when it comes to announcing a powerful God at work in public events, our silence is deafening.

The promissory covenant talks about God's action in history and in nature, not just about the "still small voice" or God's presence at times of pain or grief. As stewards of God's promissory covenant we must realize that God is a genuine actor in public events and we must learn to talk about God's active role in our world.

We back away from that. We do not want to talk about God healing one person, when thousands have not been healed. We do not want to thank God for saving us from the hurricane, earthquake, or tornado, when there were many who died. Besides, if we announce, "Lo, God is here," what happens if we find out that we were wrong? Would it not be better to run away with Jonah than prove to be a false preacher?

As Jonah found out, it does not work that way. God is a power to be reckoned with, even if we don't want to acknowledge that fact. God's promissory covenant makes God an active player on the stage of history and nature whether we desire it or not.

STEWARDSHIP

Suppose we do take seriously the theology of God's promissory covenant. Suppose we expect God's active presence in the drama of our globe, human as well as nonhuman, inanimate as well as animate. What does this mean for stewardship in theory, practice, and program? What does it mean to talk about God's promise to be unconditionally active to bless creation?

Let us begin with one important consequence of God's promissory covenant. As recipients of the divine covenant, we do not face the future alone. Solutions to the world's problems do not depend only on our skill, wisdom, or energy — not mine, not yours, not even ours together. If we can believe it, that constitutes the best news we can hear.

If we read the list of global ills equipped only with a theology that expects and even requires us to solve these problems or die, we will soon be driven to despair. Nuclear threat, toxic waste, ozone layer depletion, systemic injustice, drug addiction, etc. — the global mess is overwhelming. Even if every person on earth chose a particular issue to address — such as the preservation of an endangered species, for example — we could not solve these problems. Most of the issues are so complex and inextricably intertwined that even collectively, let alone individually, we find ourselves ineffective.

How do you respond to the experience of being overwhelmed by human and natural problems? Most North American Christians respond in one of two ways. We can decide on selective attention, concentrating our efforts on just one or two problems, and trusting that other people will take care of the issues we choose to ignore. No one individual can give time or money to every good cause. Hopefully through our combined efforts we will succeed. But do we really have the collective wisdom and ability to solve the earth's problems and so control the future?

A second common response lifts up faithfulness rather than success. We decide that God does not call us to succeed, but to be faithful. Our main goal is to hear God say to us: "Well done, good and faithful servant." It doesn't really matter if our efforts aren't successful, for we expect either that God will somehow fix everything for us or that God will take us away from this worldly mess to live in God's everlasting arms. Certainly some texts can be marshalled to support this kind of response. Nevertheless, one doubts if the Bible allows us to choose an easy faithfulness without concern for effectiveness; nor can we give up our efforts and hope that God will lift us up just before the world dies of violence or pollution.

Instead we need to rediscover what it means to take seriously God's promissory covenant. God is as urgently active in the world as we are. God has thrown the whole weight of divine skill, wisdom, and energy at this dark and deathly valley. Things can and will happen to promote life far beyond our ability to accomplish or even imagine. Our work as stewards of creation is not reducible to our efforts, individually or collectively, but is multiplied by the incredible factor of divine presence and power.

A stewardship program grounded in God's promissory covenant speaks a different language from the Mosaic covenant. Liturgically, it calls us to put aside our frantic activity and watch with wonder as Moses' words are re-enacted in each generation: "Do not be afraid, stand firm, and see the deliverance that the LORD will accomplish for you today" (Exod. 14:13). Listen to the familiar promissory language in Isaiah:

> Behold, I am doing a new thing;
>   now it springs forth, do you not perceive it?
> I will make a way in the wilderness
>   and rivers in the desert. (Isa. 43:19, RSV)

74

This prophet to Israel in exile knew the despair of the darkening valley, evil too monstrous to handle. Nevertheless he could say:

> Those who wait for the LORD shall renew their strength,
>   they shall mount up with wings like eagles,
> they shall run and not be weary,
>   they shall walk and not faint. (Isa. 40:31)

The language of Israel's poets during the Exile was almost entirely the language of God's promissory covenant. Although they did not face the same evils that we face in our modern world — the threat of nuclear holocaust comes to mind most readily — they did know homelessness and hopelessness. In their time of despair they turned to God's promissory covenant.

Liturgically the language of promissory covenant is the announcement of *shalom* in the face of suffering, whether that suffering is caused by hunger, drug abuse, or disease. Financially the language of promissory covenant is like the advice of Jeremiah's investment banker: buy land in Anathoth even though trouble has destroyed everyone's confidence in life on earth (Jer. 32). Invest your life and energy in God's promissory covenant.

Where are the real investment opportunities, the chances to join God's future? Admittedly, we may have trouble here. North American churches have done a pretty good job of convincing people that there is no divine picture, that the future we humans forecast is the only possible future. By ignoring the texts of God's promissory covenant, we have left some people scrambling alone toward an uncharted future and others hopelessly exhausted. Many have given up the office of steward, confused, burned out, or both.

The promissory covenant of Sarah, Abraham, David,

and Noah is anchored just as deep within the biblical tradition as the covenant demanding human responsibility. It is not a covenant of irresponsibility (we will look at that more in a subsequent chapter), but of hope beyond our efforts and imagination. It is not a covenant of human passivity and selfishness, but of divine presence and power.

God does not sit on a divine throne waiting for us to be good stewards. God is already at work. Our stewardship promotes the divine *shalom* initiative, which happens beyond us and even in spite of us as well as through us.

Questions for Discussion and Reflection

1. Many Christians find God's promissory covenant difficult to translate from a theological confession to an everyday reality. How do you understand the affirmation that God has unconditionally promised to work for the benefit of life on earth?

2. We live as heirs to God's promissory covenant with Noah: "I will never again curse the ground because of humankind . . . nor will I ever again destroy every living creature" (Gen. 8:21).

   a. Do you find that the promise reduces anxiety by affirming that God is unconditionally committed to life on earth?

   b. Do you find the promise troubling, even misleading, because it might promote human passivity or irresponsibility?

3. Our temptation is to try to merge the two covenant traditions together to create a hybrid, an unconditional promise that requires human accountability. Would you be a faithful steward if the covenant did not demand accountability, but simply promised God's unceasing activity promoting life on earth?

7. Joseph: Saga of Stewards

Before going on, let's take a moment to look back at the biblical material we have explored. We began by looking at Genesis 1 and 2. In those chapters we found God naming humankind as steward of the earth. The steward's job description uses the language of management and administration but also the language of service and caretaking. Fundamentally humanity assumed the responsibility to promote life on earth in the manner and image of the Creator. Such life-promoting stewardship includes all that God formed and declared "good."

In Genesis 3–11 we found stories about abuse of that trust: misuse of freedom, rivalry, caste systems, exploitation, protectionism — painful stories of stewardship gone wrong. In the middle of those narratives we saw God, torn by anger and sorrow, threatening to destroy all creation. Nevertheless, God decided to stay with the stewards, and so the story did not end there in the tower city or on the raging sea. Instead, through a promissory covenant (Gen. 9), God made a commitment to use all the divine power to promote life on earth.

In chapter 5 we turned to the covenant tradition in

77

the Bible. Like the creation mandate, covenant constitutes another way in which the Bible describes the agreement between God and the stewards concerning the promotion and enhancement of life on earth. In the covenant tradition of Moses, we found a basic biblical theology for steward-ship: The covenanting God acted to gift the stewards with life, home, and sustenance. In response the covenanting stewards promise to faithfully promote life, home, and sustenance for all the earth. This is not a small matter. The future of life on earth depends on the stewards' faithfulness.

In chapter six we traced a second tradition of covenant in the Bible, a covenant associated with Sarah and Abraham, among others. The tradition of promissory covenant features God's unconditional promise to bless creation. God does not demand any reciprocal work by the covenanting stewards. God acts as steward of the earth, directing the whole of the divine effort toward *shalom*. God's promise knows no limits — even God's own Son is sent for the life of the world.

In this chapter we will explore one particular steward-ship story in the Bible, the story of Joseph. Why Joseph? He is one of the few biblical characters officially appointed to the position of steward (Gen. 39:4). In addition, the Joseph narrative brings together all the dynamics of the steward in the Bible that we have explored. In many situations Joseph acted as a wise and faithful steward, as-suming the responsibility he should as a covenant partner. However, on other occasions the rivalry within his family clouded his judgment and compromised his stewardship. Nevertheless, as promised in the covenant, God acted to preserve life, even when the people acted to destroy.

JOSEPH, THE MODEL STEWARD

The office and activities of Joseph provide an intentional illustration in story form of what the Bible means by steward. Joseph is a steward par excellence. He functioned both as manager and as caretaker. Working as a model steward in the image of God, Joseph promoted the interests and tended the assets of his masters. Joseph's action as steward enhanced life for all those around him.

Let us look first at Joseph as steward in the house of Potiphar. We do not know the events that led to Joseph's appointment to this position. The narrator simply tells us that "the LORD was with Joseph, and he became a successful man" (Gen. 39:2). Furthermore, Potiphar recognized God's presence with Joseph and saw that the Lord caused everything that Joseph touched to "prosper in his hands" (39:3).

One might suspect that it was the "prospering" under Joseph that was the determinative factor in Potiphar's choice of the Hebrew as his steward. However, the narrative does not seem to view Potiphar in a negative or cynical light. Any "household" will prosper in the hands of a wise and faithful steward. Nor is the word "prosper" used here in a strictly economic sense. It involves more than simply a growing stock portfolio. "Prospering" involves the general welfare of the community.

The enhancement of life which God wants for all of creation really happened for Potiphar. In fact, the household prospered so magnificently that Potiphar could retire. Something like that seems to be the meaning of the final sentence of the description of Joseph's appointment: Potiphar "had no concern for anything but the food that he ate" (39:6).

We know the story well enough to remember that a crisis ended Joseph's tenure as steward in Potiphar's house-

79

hold. The master's wife tried to seduce Joseph. When her efforts proved unsuccessful, she publicly accused him of attempted rape. That accusation landed this talented steward in prison. However, even in prison Joseph proved his skill as steward. It was not long before the prison superintendent appointed Joseph steward of the prison! Apparently life in prison improved under Joseph's management. Again the text uses the word "prosper" (39:23), also noting God's presence in this success. Joseph's skillful stewarding freed the superintendent to take a vacation; the superintendent had no worry about anything he put in Joseph's hands.

Joseph's days as steward were not to end in prison. Because of Joseph's perceptiveness in interpreting dreams, he came to the attention of the Egyptian Pharaoh. Joseph warned Pharaoh that difficult days lay ahead, days of famine. Joseph recommended that someone be appointed to take charge of planning for this eventuality, a person who was both discerning and wise (41:33). Pharaoh quickly appointed a number of stewards with instructions to begin planning for famine. Then Pharaoh turned to the matter of appointing the chief steward. Not surprisingly, he chose Joseph, "one in whom is the spirit of God" (41:38).

Joseph set to work organizing the food supply during the time of good harvests so there would be food when the fields dried up. When the famine did come, it struck with a vengeance. Famine engulfed not only Egypt, but the surrounding areas as well. As the food supply dwindled, Joseph opened the storehouses. Apparently Joseph was not selfish about the grain supply: "all the world" came to Egypt to buy grain and they received food (41:57).

These episodes of the saga present Joseph as a model steward. Wherever this steward worked, life improved — in the household, the prison, and the world. After so many illustrations of unfaithful stewards and the catastrophes they created, it is a relief to relax and enjoy this story of Joseph, a steward who clearly acts in the image and spirit of God.

GOD, THE DIVINE STEWARD

According to the narrative, Joseph was not alone as steward in Egypt. The narrator has been careful to let us know that, whether in Potiphar's house, in prison, or in the palace, Joseph was accompanied by God. Certainly Joseph functioned as a wise and faithful steward, but God was a major factor in the stewardship that happened through Joseph. As the narrator says, "the LORD caused all that [Joseph] did to prosper in his hands" (39:3). When it came to the central crisis in the narrative, the famine, God's presence enabled Joseph to anticipate the coming famine. This in turn allowed Pharaoh to make plans to handle it.

However, God's work as steward in this saga is not limited to the agency of Joseph. In order to see this, we need to explore the family story that brackets and becomes entangled with the story of the Hebrew steward in Egypt. The family story begins in Genesis 37 with the disintegration of Israel's family. Joseph, the arrogant young son, sowed dissension between his older brothers and his father (37:2). He claimed to be the most important member of the family at the expense of his brothers and even his parents.

Joseph ended up sold into slavery, the victim of his brothers' plot. The brothers conspired to get rid of their insolent younger sibling and threw him into a cistern. At first they intended to leave him there to die; then it occurred to them that they could make money from this conspiracy by selling him into slavery. But before they could do so, Midianite traders came along and found Joseph; they sold him to the Ishmaelites, forcing the brothers to cover up a confusing crime.

Nor was the father without fault in this story of family self-destruction. Israel, caught by his preference for Joseph, fed the pretensions of this son by giving him a royal coat. In so doing, Israel lost the son he most wanted to preserve. At the end of the episode the family of Israel lay in rubble.

Israel's family story joins the story of Joseph in Egypt through the agency of the famine. The famine forced Israel to send his sons to Egypt to buy food. There they had to deal with Egypt's master steward, Joseph, their brother whom they did not recognize. What follows this initial meeting is not so much a struggle between Joseph and his brothers, but between Joseph and his father, Israel. The brothers functioned as the shuttle service between them. Both Israel and Joseph sought to control Benjamin, Israel because Benjamin was the last son of his favorite wife, Rachel, and Joseph because Benjamin was his only full brother. We have no idea what Benjamin wanted. He was simply a pawn between the two powerful men.

The struggle over Benjamin continued until finally, at the moment of greatest danger, when Joseph was on the verge of winning control of Benjamin — and indeed, control of his whole world — Joseph lost control of himself (45:1). From that moment on, *shalom* began to replace disintegration in the family, leading to reconciliation and reunion.

In a speech at the end of the drama, Joseph provides a theological interpretation of the events. He insists that the Great Steward had been at work through and in spite of the family meanness. God had worked to promote life for this family, but not only for this family. God had been at work for the benefit of life on earth: "God sent me before you to preserve life" (45:5).

The promissory covenant of God profoundly affects the story of Joseph. God works — often invisibly — to promote life. To be sure God worked in part through Joseph, so that we see the cooperation of the Divine Steward and the model steward. But the Joseph saga does not limit God's stewardship to such symbiotic activities. God's stewarding work in this story happens in spite of the family as well as through the family. God acted in spite of the family to preserve life on earth.

Hence the Joseph saga signals at least two ways in which we should expect to see the stewarding work of God. We will find God at work through wise and faithful human stewards. In such cooperation, God's presence will enable good to happen far beyond the wisdom and effort of any individual or community of faithful stewards. In addition, we should expect to see the Divine Steward at work in spite of the poor stewardship that goes on in the human community around and among us.

God's unconditional efforts on behalf of the created world will be visible to those who expect such divine activity. Obviously that does not mean that human sin cannot undo divine stewardship. Apparently God has given us that much power and freedom. But it does mean that God will never quit trying to preserve and enhance life for all the world's creatures, even in the face of human opposition and irresponsibility.

LAND, THE INANIMATE STEWARD

We have looked at the saga through the activities of two stewards, Joseph and God, but we are not yet finished. There is still another steward to discuss, a steward whose work is usually ignored: that steward is the land — not the people of the land, but the land itself. This character is introduced and emphasized in the very first verse of the saga: "Jacob settled in the land where his father had lived as an alien, the land of Canaan" (37:1). The "land" will play a critical role in this saga.

The story of the land begins in Canaan's northern hill country. The sons of Jacob, all except Joseph, have brought the family sheep and goats to that hill country because the land promised to care for the flocks. Joseph was sent to join his brothers, and when he arrived his brothers carried out their plot against him. But the land continued to do its life-promoting task regardless of the people's life-destroying actions. The land seldom gets much attention as steward. Normally the land goes about its stewardship tasks quietly, caring for plant, animal, and human life efficiently and effectively, but unnoticed.

When the land ceased to care for the inhabitants of the earth, then real trouble erupted. In the last verse of chapter 41 we are told that when the land quit stewarding the results were disastrous: "the famine became severe throughout the world." In this narrative the land's inactivity created the crisis that led to the healing of Israel's family.

As we noted, Joseph, Pharaoh's steward, had paid attention to the stewarding role of the earth. When the land quit working, Egypt was prepared — prepared well enough that "all the world" could be fed. To be sure, Joseph needed the help of the Divine Steward as well. But that kind of cooperation seems to be stewardship at its very best: the Divine Steward, the human steward, and the land all engaged together in the task of caring for the earth and its inhabitants.

The land plays another role in the saga in the midst of the famine, not as an active agent, but, like Benjamin, as a pawn in Joseph's effort to control life. Because of the lack of food, the Egyptians were as vulnerable as Israel's family. Joseph, not always a benevolent steward, used the Egyptians' vulnerability to extort their land (47:20), making them slaves of Pharaoh (47:25). This enslaving of the Egyptians proved to be a disastrous act of poor stewardship by Joseph. Later his descendants would cry out against their oppression by the Egyptians who in turn enslave them.

With the resumption of fertility, the land disappears from the Joseph narrative until Jacob asks to eventually be buried in his "home land" (47:30). The stewardship activity of the land resumes its usual unnoticed role. The other inanimate "stewards" in creation — water, air, and fire, for example — are equally unassuming. In general they go quietly about the task of preserving and even enhancing life on earth. We do not notice their stewardship activity until something goes wrong. Then we do notice and we try to reestablish the cooperative stewardship of the land (etc.), humankind, and God.

It might seem a bit odd to talk about a triangle of stewards: God, humankind, and the land. However, it is not unusual in the stories of our ancestors, both biblical and more contemporary. Our rural ancestors were perhaps more aware than we are of the land's stewardship of us. They could have spoken of both stewardship of the land and stewardship by the land — though they probably would not have used that language.

It may be a sign of our human-centeredness that we seldom consider that the land takes care of us just as we are responsible to take care of the land. Even so, most of us realize that the land's ability to steward us is affected by our willingness to steward the land, though it is not completely determined by our stewardship. We find a measure of grace even here. The land, the water, the air, and the other "inanimate stewards" keep trying to care for us even when we neglect or even violate them.

THE TRIANGLE OF STEWARDS

We find in the Joseph saga many of the same dynamics of stewardship that we live with each day. The triangle of stewards — divine, human, and nonhuman — continues to work together, and occasionally against each other.

Joseph acted at times like a model steward. His wisdom and action preserved and enhanced life in various arenas. Not just his family or friends but the whole world was nourished because of his stewardship. However, Joseph was not always a paragon of stewardship. His egocentric desire for control sometimes threatened to destroy community rather than enhance life.

Our world is blessed and beset by a similar mixture of faithful stewardship and destructively sinful behavior. Sometimes we search frantically for faithful stewards, seeing only the globe-threatening behavior of a self-centered humanity. But the faithful stewards are there, perhaps hidden by anonymity or overlooked in our panic. A perceptive eye will spot people who wisely live their life in concert with the whole of creation. Internally they live as an organic whole: spirit, mind, and body as one. Externally they act out a wisdom that values all of creation, human and nonhuman alike.

God continues to steward creation. Sometimes we recognize the hand of God supporting the efforts of human stewards. At other times we must echo Joseph's theology: We meant it for evil, but God acted for good so that many might be preserved (Gen. 50:20). In either case, whether God works through or in spite of us, the divine presence insures that good stewardship is not limited by our faithfulness and energy.

In addition, the nonhuman stewards care for life. The water and air have their own ways of purification and renewal so that they can enhance life on earth. To be sure, they struggle to keep up with our efforts to pollute them, but they never give up. The soil and its vegetation continue their efforts to nourish life. They even try to force their way through the asphalt with which we bury them. The nonhuman animals try to establish a balance that promotes life for all. Often it proves difficult due to human interference. But we too are a part of their web of life, and they will include us in their stewardship efforts if we are willing to join them.

The Joseph narrative is not the only stewardship story in the Bible, but it presents a particularly helpful canonical portrait of stewardship as we have explored it throughout this study. The stewardship role of people (faithful and unfaithful), the covenant of gift and responsibility, and the promissory covenant are all featured in this one biblical saga, just as they are in our own lives. Hopefully, looking closely at this narrative will help us to see how the same dynamics of biblical stewardship play themselves out in our life stories.

Questions for Discussion and Reflection

1. The saga presents Joseph as a model of wise and faithful stewardship. Who comes to your mind when you think of a model steward? What are the marks of a good steward?

2. In the previous chapter we looked at God's promissory covenant, that is, stewardship which does not depend on human agency. Now we have read a narrative in which God's promissory stewardship happens not in a dramatic, interruptive way, but as a part of the normal flow of events. Can you identify times when actions may have been "meant for evil," but God acted to promote life?

3. How is the "natural" world acting to promote life on earth? We may need to turn to natural scientists (zoologists, geologists, etc.) to help us better understand some of the stewardship efforts of rocks, animals, water, and air. Farmers and botanists can teach us a great deal about the soil and vegetation as stewards.

8. Let the Rivers Run

People become a unified community when they share the same story. Hence there may have been no more important people in ancient Israel than the storytellers. They had the task of gathering up as many of the community tales as possible and forming out of them a common story which included everyone. The story they told in the village squares, in homes, and in the sanctuaries was not just a story about a specific people's efforts and foibles; it was also a theological story, a divine drama. It was a tale about God, who gave birth to this people, broke the chains that bound them, and gave to them a land flowing with possibilities and problems.

The magnificence of this great story is displayed in the fact that it not only became the narrative of this peculiar people in a particular place, but it also has the power to include all people, even to our day. The community of faith gradually came to realize that God was the power and inspiration behind this great story.

In the previous chapters we have looked at specific sections of this great story, exploring the person of the steward, a metaphor which arises from the story itself. In this final chapter we shall focus more specifically on the work of the steward, using another biblical metaphor: river.

Rivers play an important role in the biblical story. In addition to being a geographical entity, a river has symbolic theological import related to fertility, community, and the promise of new life. Hence as we try to summarize the work of the biblical steward we will follow three rivers: the rivers of creation, the river of justice and righteousness, and the river Jordan.

THE RIVERS OF CREATION

In the drama of creation found in Genesis 2, the earth exists first as a vast desert, sterile for lack of rain. The land needed a river to water it and bring it to life (2:6), so God caused a river to flow out of Eden to water the garden, earth (2:10). In fact, this creation river divided so that it flowed to all the known parts of the globe. From these rivers the lush garden earth received the water it needed to sustain and promote life.

Our task as the earth's stewards has been to let these rivers of creation run. God gave life-sustaining fertility to the earth. We have been given the opportunity and the power to channel the natural resources of this garden to energetically enhance life on earth. As we know, not all has gone well. We have not used God's creation rivers to enhance life in the garden. Instead we have used the air, water, and soil to promote life for certain creatures on earth. Most generally, we have used the earth's natural resources to foster human life. We have seldom even considered that the rivers of creation are to run for the benefit of nonhuman and even inanimate life on earth, as well as for humanity.

We do not even consider the whole human community in our use of natural resources. We have decided that the rivers of creation are primarily to benefit this generation — in other words, us. Only recently and occasionally have we realized that it is our task, as stewards of creation's rivers, to let them run for our children and their children and their children. Our anxiety rises only when we realize that chemicals may be poisoning our water, that the wind may be blowing away our soil, or that trapped heat may be changing our climate. We are only beginning to understand that even miracle cures will not be enough to rescue the next generation if we use up all the rivers and rain forests of creation.

Even within this generation we do not assume that the rivers run for everyone. Our decisions betray our conviction that some stewards deserve more access to the earth's natural resources than others. Furthermore, our wastefulness indicates that we assume an unlimited supply of life-giving water, air, soil, and energy. No matter how wise we feel we are, it is very difficult to realize that the rivers of creation may not be able to sustain life at the levels some of us hope for. At any rate, we have trouble stewarding so that all life on earth can drink together from the rivers of creation. Instead, some have the opportunity to drink freely and others struggle with more or less constant thirst.

As stewards working in the image of God, we have been entrusted with the task of using the earth's resources to promote life for all and for as long as the earth shall last. There are good signs that we are beginning to look at our stewarding task as it extends beyond this generation. Steps are being taken — sometimes reluctantly, sometimes with a rush of enthusiasm — to ensure an adequate supply of air, water, soil, and fuel for the next generation. Such stewarding work cannot be accomplished in a rush of news headlines. It requires the lifelong work and commitment of all stewards. Nevertheless, we welcome an increased general awareness that it takes all of us working together to let the rivers run for the next generation.

While we have become more aware of the need to exercise stewardship on behalf of future generations, we have been somewhat less interested in the immediate problems of stewarding the earth's resources for all human life on earth, let alone the nonhuman life. So far human management of the earth has resulted in some people living very well while others live very poorly. We have yet to discover the common quality of life that could be enjoyed by all equally if we worked to enhance life on all the globe. As individuals, we struggle to address both the needs of those close to us and the sometimes more desperate needs of people in other parts of the world. Too often we see some people working to promote life on distant parts of the globe but overlooking the needs of their own families and communities, while others foster an opulent life-style for themselves and those closest to them, ignoring the effect that has on the rest of the world.

We have been appointed stewards of all the earth; we have been given the task of managing the earth's resources for the benefit of all human and nonhuman life on this globe for today and unending tomorrows. We can feel such stewardship responsibility as an unbelievable burden. However, we need to remember that God has already set the rivers to run and that God continues to perpetuate their motion. Our task does not require us to create the "water," but simply to channel the resources already present. In other words, as stewards of creation we must simply let the rivers continue to run.

THE RIVER OF RIGHTEOUSNESS

The prophet Amos uses "river" as a poetic image in one of the Bible's best-known cries for justice:

> I hate, I despise your festivals,
> and I take no delight in your solemn assemblies.
> . . . .
> Take away from me the noise of your songs;
> I will not listen to the melody of your harps.
> But let justice roll down like waters,
> and righteousness like an everflowing stream.
> (Amos 5:21-24)

The geography of Canaan was and is cut by dry stream beds and deep gorges. Water flows in these fickle rivers only during heavy rainstorms, so these rivers cannot be counted on to sustain life, either animal or vegetable. Apparently Amos found in these rivers, which destructively gush and then disastrously dry up, an apt analogy for the human relationships in the community around him. Amos realized that the behavior he observed in the sanctuary, palace, and marketplace could not sustain Israel's life much longer. Israel would soon self-destruct under the weight of its own injustice and unrighteousness. God's judgment could be seen in this impending collapse of Israel.

In sixth century B.C.E. Israel, justice and righteousness had become a word pair "slogan" for the interpersonal relationships of a healthy community (cf. Psalm 72). The Hebrew words which we translate "justice and righteousness" do not refer only to fair behavior and proper piety, as they sometimes do in our vocabulary. Certainly the two words do not expect less than such fairness, but they call for much more.

This word pair describes a community, large or small,

in which all members work for the benefit of one another and for the community as a whole. Obviously every community has some members who are strong and others who are less strong, some who are wealthy and others who are not. The weaker and poorer members of the community are at risk. Their welfare depends on the justice and righteousness of the community's leaders. Without that quality of community interaction, the life of these "at risk" members is diminished and shortened. Israel's prophets mention several categories of disadvantaged members, including the poor, the widow, the orphan, and the alien. These categories represent very real groups of people in ancient Israel, but they also function symbolically in the prophetic poetry. They include all those within the village or country who are unable to sustain their own life without assistance from others.

In a community in which interactions reflect "justice and righteousness," the economic, religious, and social strength of all helps to sustain the life of those who are less able to sustain their own lives. Amos saw around him the economic power of the community used to trample the poor and needy (8:4-6). The social power of the community functioned to oppress the powerless and crush the needy (4:1). Yet the religious festivals of the community paraded on as if nothing was wrong (5:21-23). Such a community is doomed to self-destruct under divine judgment (7:7-9).

We have been appointed stewards of the river of righteousness. It is not hard to find in our communities, local and global, the same decay that ate away sixth-century Israel. Sometimes the pervasive presence of injustice and unrighteousness seems to make them the norm. We find ourselves burdened by the knowledge that even the clothes we wear have been made in shops and factories that intentionally oppress those members of society who are at risk. We feel paralyzed by the realization that injustice so infects our life that no action we take can be entirely free of contamination.

God offers two items of good news designed to lift the paralysis and lighten the burden. In the first place, a river of divine activity carries justice and righteousness. When we act justly and rightly we are moving with the wave of history, not against it. Injustice requires us to paddle upstream. Unrighteousness eventually runs aground. Somehow we have become so distorted that we actually believe that injustice is natural. We assume that justice only exists because of our superhuman efforts.

Admittedly contamination by the virus of injustice has eliminated any dreams of a "noble savage." We cannot somehow return people to a pristine state where all would be righteous. Nevertheless, we do not have to generate justice and righteousness out of nothing. We know what is good and right. Examples of justice happen around us all the time in families, in churches, in local communities, and even beyond. Justice is available to roll down like waters, and righteousness like an everflowing stream, if we but let the rivers run.

Secondly, as Christians we know that we have been freed from the debilitating paralysis of our history of injustice. All our exhausting efforts to control life for our personal gain have failed. The residue of such futility scars the landscape and our own soul. Through Christ, God has given us a chance to start over without carrying the baggage of our past behavior and our learned inclinations. We have not been freed to continue the injustice of the past, but to float on the river of righteousness.

We participate in the church, a community of people who have committed themselves to be a part of that river. Occasionally one or many of us "bail out" and have to be shown again the direction of the current. As we act justly and do right, life does spring forth from the sterile deserts around. We find ourselves spending less time and energy fighting against the hate that surrounds us, and more in joining the explosion of vitality, fertility, and community that bursts out when the poor, widows, orphans, and aliens receive the nourishment they need. Injustice and fighting against injustice will consume incredible amounts of energy and will drain all our resources if we let it. Doing justice and righteousness multiplies energy and promotes creativity. As with the rivers of creation, so also with the river of righteousness, we live the abundant life God intends when we let the rivers run.

THE RIVER JORDAN

No river gained more symbolic significance in the biblical tradition than the river Jordan. As a geographical entity, the Jordan does not rank among the top rivers of the world. It is relatively short, in many places quite narrow, and most of the way very brackish. However, it is the river of ancient Israel, meandering from the Sea of Galilee to the Dead Sea at the bottom of the deep geological fault known in that area as the Jordanian rift. The importance of the river Jordan lies in its theological significance. Hence in the biblical tradition it becomes the mighty Jordan.

In the story of Joshua, the Jordan serves as the entrance to the land of God's promise. God appointed Joshua as steward of the Jordan, the one designated to lead the people through the river to their promised home. The narrative reports that as Joshua stood at the edge of the river, he heard God speak. God's exhortation concluded with a word of assurance:

I hereby command you: Be strong and courageous; do not be frightened or dismayed, for the LORD your God is with you wherever you go. (Josh. 1:9)

After Joshua had made the necessary preparations, all Israel gathered at the edge of the river. The story records that the priests carrying the ark of Yahweh were the first to enter the river. When they stepped into the water, the Jordan ceased its flow and all Israel crossed over into God's promised land (Josh. 3:14-17). Just as Israel had crossed from bondage to freedom through water by divine design, so now they crossed from wandering to home through the Jordan.

The Jordan was the site of an important new beginning on another occasion as well. Jesus stood at the edge of the Jordan at the beginning of his ministry. According to Matthew, John the Baptist was reluctant to baptize Jesus, feeling that he should be baptized by Jesus instead. Jesus in turn responds, "Let it be so now; for it is proper for us in this way to fulfill all righteousness" (Matt. 3:15). Jesus, like Israel before him, passed through the river Jordan into the life God had promised and to the work God had appointed. In Luke's account, after attending to his own spiritual health, Jesus began to work (Luke 4:14-15). Through word and touch, the Teacher/Physician called others to cross the Jordan into God's promised life and to work as stewards of the good news of the Jordan.

We have been appointed stewards not only of the rivers of creation and righteousness but also of the river Jordan. In the words of Paul to the Corinthians, we are "stewards of God's mysteries" (1 Cor. 4:1). Many of us find it difficult to be stewards of the river Jordan; we are uncomfortable with our responsibility to show the river to others and invite them to cross it. We find it more comfortable to be stewards of creation or justice, waxing eloquent and working diligently on behalf of the environment or disadvantaged people at home and abroad. Instead of striving to be responsible stewards of all three rivers — the Jordan as well as the rivers of creation and righteousness — we often choose to criticize those who reduce Christian stewardship to evangelism alone, using this often valid criticism as a technique to avoid our own evangelistic responsibilities, because we do not really want to be stewards of the Jordan.

We cannot have it both ways. To be sure, we are frequently justified in objecting to the behavior of many who focus on bringing people to Christ. Christian stewardship involves much more than only inviting people to enter the promised land. And sometimes wild and unchristian promises of prosperity and perfection accompany the invitation to cross over Jordan. We ought to object to such practices.

Nevertheless, we cannot object to poor stewardship but refuse to tend the Jordan ourselves. Christian stewardship does include the role of Joshua, leading people through the Jordan into the promised land. Stewardship involves caring for both earthly and spiritual needs. Some who are homeless need shelter for their bodies and others need it for their souls. Some who are lost need a map of the city and others need a map of the City of God. We cannot just avoid our responsibility, ignoring those who wander aimlessly through life, unable to orient themselves because no one has invited them to cross the river Jordan.

As stewards of the mysteries of God, we know the comfort and the challenge of the waters of Jordan. That river is available to soothe the pain of the world, to wash away the dirt of life, and to direct the currents of history. We do not have to hunt for the river. It is at hand. We do not need to jump start the river. It always runs. Our task as stewards of the river Jordan is to show the river to others, invite them to cross over to the life God has promised, and let the river run.

STEWARDS OF GOD'S RIVERS

The rivers of creation, the river of righteousness, and the river Jordan have been given by God as promise and responsibility. As promise, they flow as a gift from God. We human stewards do not carry the weight of creation. God works through nature to renew life on earth. The soil cleanses the water. The water brings vegetation from the earth. The vegetation replenishes the oxygen. The sun furnishes the power. So the rivers of creation run.

In the same way, we do not have to generate justice and righteousness out of nothing. God has written justice and righteousness into the very fabric of community life. Injustice eventually self-destructs, though often this brings much pain to both the just and the unjust. Righteousness brings the satisfaction of giving and receiving, loving and being loved. We need only the wisdom to discern righteousness and the courage to do justice. Inexorably the river runs.

Likewise, through story, tradition, and ritual, we receive the river Jordan. The promise of new life stands as sure as God and as visible as our own experience. We do not need to build God's promised land; we need only to invite people to enter. The Jordan flows on, waiting for people to cross over.

Nevertheless, responsibility comes with these rivers which flow as a gift from God. We have the responsibility to let the rivers run. Creation groans under the mismanagement of foolish stewards. We must stop throwing the trash of our abuse into the rivers of creation. We must stop erecting dams to direct the rivers' flow only to our use, so that they water only this generation. We have become the enemies of the rivers of creation; we must become stewards of the rivers once again.

Just as Israel under Egyptian bondage and the early church under Roman persecution cried out because of their suffering, so the oppressed continue to cry out today. The river of righteousness will wash us away with the unjust if we continue to turn a deaf ear to those cries. As stewards of the river of righteousness we can change the course of history by doing justice and calling others to account.

As stewards of the Jordan, we must not be ashamed of the gospel. Recent efforts to be accepting of all people have made some Christians hesitant to talk about new life in Christ. These efforts may constitute an appropriate response to the narrow religious bigotry that has characterized some segments of the Christian tradition. Nevertheless, we cannot use a theology of "tolerance" as an excuse to avoid our responsibility as stewards of the mysteries of God. Even if others have chosen to follow other religious streams, we know what lies across the Jordan.

Questions for Discussion and Reflection

1. What changes have you made in your life-style in the past five or ten years in order to be a more faithful steward of the rivers of creation? What environmental danger concerns you most as a threat to the fertility of God's garden for the next generation? What steps do you need to take?

2. Issues of justice and righteousness confront us each day. Can you identify situations which have become more just and right

in the past year or decade? We do not always agree as to what justice demands in every given situation. What are the issues in your congregation or home about which faithful stewards disagree?

3. Christians regularly differ in manner and approach as stewards of the river Jordan. How would you describe your style of evangelism? Are you satisfied as well as comfortable with it? How can we be energetic stewards of the mysteries of God and at the same time avoid being bigoted and intolerant of other religious perspectives?

Selected Bibliography

Austin, Richard C. *Hope for the Land: Nature in the Bible.*
Atlanta: John Knox Press, 1988.

Birch, Bruce C., and Larry L. Rasmussen. *The Predicament of
the Prosperous.* Philadelphia: Westminster Press, 1978.

Brattgard, Helge. *God's Stewards.* Trans. G. Lund. Minneapolis: Augsburg, 1963.

Brueggemann, Walter. *The Land.* Philadelphia: Fortress Press,
1977.

Brueggemann, Walter, Sharon Parks, and Thomas Groome.
*To Act Justly, Love Tenderly, Walk Humbly: An Agenda for
Ministers.* New York: Paulist Press, 1986.

Granberg-Michaelson, Wesley. *A Worldly Spirituality: The Call to
Redeem Life on Earth.* San Francisco: Harper & Row, 1984.

Granberg-Michaelson, Wesley, ed. *Tending the Garden.* Grand
Rapids: Eerdmans, 1987.

Gunneweg, A. H. J., and W. Schmithals. *Achievement.* Nashville: Abingdon Press, 1981.

Hall, Douglas John. *Imaging God: Dominion as Stewardship.*
Grand Rapids: Eerdmans, 1986.

————. *The Steward: A Biblical Symbol Come of Age.* Revised
edition. Grand Rapids: Eerdmans, 1990.

————. *The Stewardship of Life in the Kingdom of Death*. Grand Rapids: Eerdmans, 1985.

Kantonen, T. A. *A Theology for Christian Stewardship*. Philadelphia: Muhlenberg Press, 1956.

McCarthy, D. J. *Old Testament Covenant*. Richmond, VA: John Knox Press, 1975.

McComiskey, T. E. *The Covenants of Promise*. Grand Rapids: Baker Book House, 1985.

McFague, Sallie. *Models of God: Theology for an Ecological, Nuclear Age*. Philadelphia: Fortress Press, 1987.

Merchant, Carolyn. *The Death of Nature: Women, Ecology, and the Scientific Revolution*. San Francisco: Harper & Row, 1980.

Moltmann, Jürgen. *God in Creation*. San Francisco: Harper & Row, 1985.

Murphy, Nordan C., ed. *Teaching and Preaching Stewardship*. New York: Friendship Press, 1985.

Nelson, Richard D. *First and Second Kings*. Interpretation. Atlanta: John Knox Press, 1987.

Nicholson, E. W. *God and His People*. Oxford: Clarendon Press, 1986.

Petry, Ronald D. *Partners in Creation*. Elgin, IL: The Brethren Press, 1980.

Powell, Luther P. *Money and the Church*. New York: Association Press, 1962.

Roop, Eugene F. *Genesis*. Believers Church Bible Commentary. Scottdale, PA: Herald Press, 1987.

Santmire, H. Paul. *The Travail of Nature: The Ambiguous Ecology Promise of Christian Theology*. Philadelphia: Fortress Press, 1985.

Sittler, Joseph. "Christian Theology and the Environment," in *Essays on Nature and Grace*. Philadelphia: Fortress Press, 1972.

Stackhouse, Max L. *Public Theology and Political Economy*. Grand Rapids: Eerdmans, 1987.

Steck, Odil H. *World and Environment.* Nashville: Abingdon Press, 1980.

Swenson, Joanne. "Neither the Liberal nor the Conservative God Is Adequate." *Bible Review* 5, 5 (Oct. 1989): 14-15.

Thomas, Winburn T. *Stewardship in Mission.* Englewood Cliffs, NJ: Prentice Hall, 1964.

Thompson, T. K., ed. *Stewardship in Contemporary Life.* New York: Association Press, 1965.

———. *Stewardship in Theology.* New York: Association Press, 1960.

Vallet, Ronald E. *Stepping Stones of the Steward.* Grand Rapids: Eerdmans, 1989.

Walsh, J. P. M. *The Mighty from their Thrones: Power in the Biblical Tradition.* Philadelphia: Fortress Press, 1987.

Westerhoff, John H. *Building God's People in a Materialistic Society.* New York: Seabury Press, 1983.

Westermann, Claus. *Genesis 1–11.* Minneapolis: Augsburg, 1984.

———. *Genesis 12–36.* Minneapolis: Augsburg, 1985.

———. *Genesis 37–50.* Minneapolis: Augsburg, 1986.

Index of Names and Subjects

Index of Scripture References